John Ruffini

Carlino and other Stories

John Ruffini

Carlino and other Stories

ISBN/EAN: 9783742806864

Manufactured in Europe, USA, Canada, Australia, Japa

Cover: Foto ©Andreas Hilbeck / pixelio.de

Manufactured and distributed by brebook publishing software
(www.brebook.com)

John Ruffini

Carlino and other Stories

COLLECTION
OF
BRITISH AUTHORS

TAUCHNITZ EDITION.

VOL. 1243.

CARLINO AND OTHER STORIES BY JOHN RUFFINI.

IN ONE VOLUME.

TAUCHNITZ EDITION.
By the same Author,

LAVINIA . . . . In 2 vols.
DOCTOR ANTONIO . . . . In 1 vol.
LORENZO BENONI . . . . In 1 vol.
VINCENZO . . . . In 2 vols.
A QUIET NOOK . . . . . In 1 vol.
THE PARAGREENS . . . . In 1 vol.

CARLINO

AND OTHER STORIES.

BY

JOHN RUFFINI,
AUTHOR OF "DOCTOR ANTONIO," ETC.

COPYRIGHT EDITION.

LEIPZIG
BERNHARD TAUCHNITZ
1872.

CONTENTS.

	PAGE
CARLINO	9
A CONTEMPORARY HOBBY	167
SANREMO REVISITED	187
A DESIGNING ARISTOCRAT	227
A DEED OF DARKNESS	247
A MODEST CELEBRITY	265

CARLINO.

CARLINO.

CHAPTER I.

On a stormy August morning of 1853 Baron Gaston de Kerdiat, an arrival of the night before at the Hôtel de l'Europe, Chambery, stepped from his room into the adjoining gallery, which runs along three sides of the house, leant on the rail of the balustrades, lighted a cigar and puffed away moodily at it.

Baron Gaston, a man about forty, a customer of the Hôtel de l'Europe of twenty years' standing, was not exacting, paid his bill without demur or observation, did not grudge the waiters their fees; and yet the Baron was not popular with the household. Indeed, even that best of souls, Madame Ferrolliet, the elderly landlady, who had known him from the time he was a youth of eighteen, and to whom he always made a point of being civil—well, even this good lady could not help a nervous sinking of the heart whenever the Baron's arrival was announced. As to the servants, their sensations were clear and decided—they could not bear the sight of him. His stern visage, his taciturnity, his frigid manners—he had never in all these twenty years given the landlady a shake of the hand—the entire absence, in short, of that cordiality to which all the old frequenters of the hotel, high and low, had accustomed her; all this might account for the want of sympathetic feeling evinced by the hostess towards this old customer.

But the servants, who knew their station too well to lay claim to much ceremony, what had he done to them to arouse their unlimited antipathy? Was he in the habit of finding fault with, or of using them harshly? Not at all. It would have been better had he done so, for even harsh treatment and scolding might have been construed into an acknowledgment— an odd one to be sure—but still a sort of acknowledgment, that he and they were fellow-creatures; while, as it was, waiters and chambermaids felt as though lowered to the level of things. In fact it was less what he did than what he did not that galled them beyond endurance; it was his taking, save in strict matters of service, no notice of them whatever, his overlooking them, his ignoring their being. Not a nod of recognition on arriving, not a nod of farewell at parting,—the very fee he gave them was left with Madame Ferrolliet. His orders, sparingly given, not seldom only by gestures, generally without even looking at the person from whom the service was demanded, were given to the generic waiter—never to the individual Paul or Peter. One or two unlucky fellows, new hands in the hotel, who had presumed to address him unchallenged, had received for their pains such a frown and such a stare as had taken from them all wish to repeat the experiment. A man in whom pride amounted almost to a disease, Baron Gaston de Kerdiat belonged to the same school as that lady of the old *régime* who dressed in the presence of her footman, on the assumption that a valet was not a man. Servants, in this gentleman's eyes, were not men, but useful flesh-and-blood machines to be had for hire, and so long as he paid them that hire, he considered himself quits with them. Had the question been put to him, whether he believed servants to have souls, he would have been puzzled to answer. Certainly he used them as though they had none.

This absurd system was not of the Baron's own invention, nor, I suspect, of that of the lady of the *ancien régime* just mentioned. The Baron had found it established and acted upon in his home, and had continued its practice. Perhaps, had he chosen any other career than that of arms, he might have met with such difficulties in its application as might have led to its modification. But our Baron had been in the army from 1830 to 1848, had always had soldiers for servants, and with men fashioned by iron discipline into machines, the machine system had succeeded very well.

This experience of eighteen years was so unanswerably conclusive in favour of the excellence of his method, that when it seemed to fail, as it did as soon as he adopted the life of a civilian, and could only choose his servants from among civilians, he attributed the failure rather to the wickedness of a whole class, or to his ill-luck, than to the faultiness of the principle upon which he had acted so long; and instead of changing his ways changed his servants, which was the case, on an average, every second month during the five years intervening between 1848 and 1853. It was in 1848 that he had returned to the life of a civilian. On the same day on which the second republic was proclaimed in France Baron Gaston resigned his commission, sacrificing a brilliant career, and his right to a handsome pension in a few years, to what he conceived to be his duty to his name, to his political creed, and to his royal master.

The first republic, it must be known, had brought about the ruin of the family from which he sprung, one of the oldest and wealthiest families of La Vendée. Most of its numerous members had perished either on the scaffold or in encounters with the "Blues." His ancestral château had been razed to the ground, his ancestral lands laid waste, whole villages of his destroyed; and what fire and sword had spared had been sold as national property. No wonder that the Baron abominated the reality—nay, the word descriptive of that reality, in the name of which his family had been exterminated, and himself reduced to poverty.

The gallery of the Hôtel de l'Europe overlooked the yard, and as at that moment, owing to the bad weather, it was empty, the only scope for the Baron's observation was the rain pouring down in torrents. The only living object in view, dimly distinguishable through the descending sheets of water, was a young man on the other side of the gallery, exactly opposite to where the Baron mused and smoked. This young man, from his occupation, was evidently a servant, for, in fact, he was busy brushing, one after the other, a heap of clothes lying on a chair by his side. He performed this task with a conscientiousness rarely evinced by a domestic, every now and then subjecting some article already put aside to a fresh examination, and adding what was probably a supererogatory brushing. It was a pleasure to see with what tender care he folded coats, waistcoats, and pantaloons, and laid them on a second chair with as much caution and gentleness as though they had been so many babies. All the while he was whistling, *sotto voce*, an air from the *Trovatore*. As soon, however, as he caught sight of the Baron, which he did during one of his brushing evolutions, he stopped whistling, and proving himself as respectful as conscientious, he so arranged his chairs as to avoid the necessity of turning his back on his opposite neighbour,—an attention which was quite lost on that gentleman.

A more good-natured countenance than that exhibited by this young man it would be difficult to conceive. It was in the highest degree frank and open, and Nature had stereotyped on it a smile of good-humour and good-will, which it was impossible not to notice, and once having noticed, not to sympathise with. Indeed, the milk of human kindness must have stood at boiling-point with him, not to have been frozen by the stern aspect and knitted brows of the Baron. On the contrary, he seemed rather attracted than repulsed, for, between one brushing and the other, he cast a sympathetic glance at his moody *vis-à-vis;* nay, after a little, having thus prepared the way, he hazarded in the same direction a slight motion of the head, accompanied by a deprecating look at the sky, as much as to say—Did you ever see such weather?

Baron de Kerdiat was so far from dreaming that such a liberty could be taken with him, that he looked over his shoulder in search of the person telegraphed to, and seeing no one, turned sharply round and stared fiercely at the presumptuous young fellow, who, in his simplicity, conjecturing from the stare that the meaning of his pantomime had not been understood, attempted to make it more explicit by pointing with his fingers to the lowering heavens, and with an apologetic smile said, "What weather!"

The Baron, with a furious frown, started from his leaning posture, drew himself up to his full height, his chin elevated sideways, as if in defiance, an habitual gesture with him when displeased—and God knows what he was going to say or do in vindication of his offended dignity, when happily at that moment a heavy loaded diligence rattled into the yard with a deafening noise, and the interest afforded by so important an event put an end, for the time being, to all hostility. Instantly the whole household, armed with umbrellas, was astir round the huge machine; men, women, children—a full cargo—were helped out of the interior and the rotunda, and safely landed on dry ground, but nobody troubled themselves about the *coupé*. Had the *conducteur* forgotten that there was a passenger in the *coupé*, an old lady with hair as white as snow? She had managed with great difficulty to open the door, and stood now with one foot on the steps, a picture of helplessness and perplexity. The Baron who had, from the first, followed the movements of this lady with a certain anxiety, perceiving her awkward and somewhat dangerous predicament, shouted from the gallery, "Look to the lady in the *coupé!* Somebody help her!"

The order was no sooner given than, as if by

magic, it was already obeyed. The Baron's words had scarcely been pronounced, when the squire of the brush, as though he had flown thither, was at the door of the *coupé*, had lifted out the old lady, and, under cover of his open umbrella, had carried her bodily into the house. All this had been done in a twinkling with a care and a gentleness, of which only an eye-witness could form an idea. "Very good," thought the Baron, "the man can do something better than grin at his superiors." And the gentleman's heart relented towards the offender. The lady in question, be it remembered, was an entire stranger to the Baron. Her title to his interest was her age and her silver hair. Hard and stern as he was, there was nevertheless a soft spot in his heart, the spot on which was enshrined the sacred memory of the faithful friend and stay of his youth, of her who had replaced his mother, too soon lost, alas!—the memory of his aged grandmother. All old ladies with white locks reminded him of this, his second parent, and for her sake were sacred in his eyes.

At half-past twelve, the usual dinner hour, the Baron took his place at the *table-d'hôte*, and on leaving the dining-room, went, as was his wont, to the bureau, or counting-house, where Madame Ferrolliet used to sit, to pay his bill and say good-bye before departing. He never stopped long at the hotel—arriving in the evening, he generally left on the following afternoon in the diligence for Bonneville, the same which had arrived so seasonably that morning.

"By-the-bye," said the Baron, as he turned to leave the room, "could you recommend me a good servant?"

"Yes," said Madame, "not only a good, but an excellent one."

"Ah! is he a Savoyard?"

"No; a Piedmontese."

The Baron puckered up his nostrils like one affronted by a bad smell.

"When a Piedmontese is good," continued Madame, "I assure you he's not so by half."

"May be so, but I want a Savoyard."

"I am sorry for Carlino's sake; our late Prefect, who was also a Piedmontese, could never say enough in praise of his honesty and intelligence. He placed unlimited confidence in Carlino, indeed treated him more like a friend than a servant."

"That alone would deter me from taking your *protégé*. He would not suit me. It is my habit to treat a servant as a servant, and not as a friend," said the Baron, dryly.

"Ah! well, I am very sorry for Carlino," repeated the landlady.

"Since you think so highly of him, why don't you engage him yourself?"

"I should be glad to do so, but he objects to remaining in Chambery; he has been offered a good situation in more than one family, but since his master's death, which occurred here quite unexpectedly, the poor fellow cannot bear the town."

"If this Carlino be the person that I suppose, I must say that he looks anything but inconsolable."

"Nevertheless he is so, I can assure you; by nature he is lively and good-humoured, but only name his late master to him, and see if his eyes do not fill with tears. He longs to leave this to see more of the world. I have kept him here up to this time, hoping to find him a situation such as he wishes."

Monsieur le Baron hoped she would succeed in this as in everything else, and took his leave.

At a couple of hours from Chambery on the Bonneville road lies the village of Castex, and a few hundred paces farther on rises in view, isolated on a hillock, a huge square building surrounded by vineyards. It is called in the neighbourhood, we suppose by courtesy, "The Castle." The Baron and his portmanteau were put down at the gate of this mansion. This was the goal of his present, as it had been for nearly the quarter of a century of all his visits to Savoy. The Castle was owned and inhabited by his paternal uncle, the Vidame of Kerdiat, a gentleman now past eighty years of age. This uncle and nephew were the only extant representatives of the once numerous and flourishing family of Kerdiat, and consequently set a high value on one another. From the ceremony of their manners, when together, you might have supposed them to be two dethroned princes. The Baron professed the highest reverence for the Vidame, inasmuch as he was the head of the family. The Vidame on his side respected in the Baron the heir-presumptive of the family, and the restorer that was to be of its fortunes. All which reverence and respect did not prevent their boring each other to death, an effect which greatly helped to abridge the Baron's visits. The tie between them was that of family pride, not of family affection.

The Vidame's story is soon told. Having a club foot, and rendered unfit thereby for the army, he emigrated in 1792, being then only twenty years of age. He chose Savoy as his place of voluntary exile, and followed the fallen fortunes of the house of that name until their restoration in 1815. He then returned to France. Like most emigrants, he had forgotten nothing, learned little, and fancied in his elation that the return of the legitimate branch of the Bourbons to the throne implied the return of each and all of its adherents to their ancient privileges, dignities, and fortunes. In this he was soon undeceived, as it was only with the greatest difficulty that out of the *milliard* of indemnity assigned to emigrants, he succeeded in having allotted to the family of which he was the representative a few hundred thousand francs, a sum, in fact, not equal to what had once been their yearly income. However, he pocketed the money—necessity has no law—and shook the dust of his ungrateful country off his shoes. He went back to Savoy, paid his debts, and bought the Castle and its grounds. From that time his temper grew sour, and he took to satirising friends and foes; legitimists, quasi-legitimists, the second republic, and the second empire all had their turn. He became, in short, a sort of Talleyrand *au petit pied*—certainly, like his model, he made no secret of his contempt for mankind. Just now, the chief objective, as the Germans would say, of his satire was Victor Emmanuel and his Italian aspirations. Now and then, by way of variety, he would treat his nephew to a bird's-eye view of the family splendours, count castles, villages, and steeples, describe the fêtes given on the occasion of the Dauphin's birth, &c. Lately he often repeated the same stories, and had grown rather confused as to names and dates; not much wonder at his age.

After three weeks or so of this diet our Baron had had enough of it, and took his departure. His efforts to find a servant in the adjoining village had been unavailing; two or three heavy clumsy fellows had applied for the situation, whose appearance alone would have been an insurmountable objection, even had they in all other respects suited the Baron. And so he would have to go as he came, that is, without

a servant; and this vexed him not a little. The Vidame
improved the occasion to read him, in his usual cyni-
cal tone, a lecture on this topic. "The seed of good
servants," pronounced the old gentleman, "is lost, as
well as that of many other good things. You will
find nothing of the kind, neither under this latitude
or that. Servants nowadays, whatever their nationality
—Savoyards, French, Italian, Poles, or Belgians—are
all alike thieves, and scoundrels, and the born enemies
of their masters to boot. The safest plan is to hire
the cleverest you can pick up—a clever man is more
likely than a stupid one to plunder you *cum sale dis-
cretionis*, in order to make his gains last longer; 'Pelar
la quaglia, e nonla far gridare' ('to plume the quail
without making it cry'), as the Italians say, who are
masters in that sort of trade."

Whether owing to this tirade, or the result of reflection alien to it, thus far it is certain, that the first
thing the Baron did on reaching the Hôtel de l'Europe,
was to go to Madame Ferrolliet's parlour, and after
the customary inquiry about her health, to ask if her
protégé was still in the house. The answer being in
the affirmative, he then begged her to send Carlino
to his room within the next half-hour.

The newly-arrived traveller was stooping over his
open portmanteau with his back to the door, when
there came a gentle rap, and upon a sonorous *Entrez*,
in came on tiptoe, smiling good-naturedly, our squire

of the brush, a wiry, middle-sized, well-figured young man of five-and-twenty. Not handsome, but agreeable-looking, Carlino had none of the marked characteristics of an Italian; his complexion was clear, his eye hazel, his hair chestnut. The Baron glanced at him from over his shoulder, perceiving which the Italian hastened to make a profound obeisance. Taking no notice of it, the Frenchman resumed the review of the contents of his trunk.

After a pause, and without changing posture, he said curtly, "You are looking for a situation, and wish to leave Savoy, I am told."

"Yes, Monsieur le Baron; and I shall consider myself very fortun——"

"Do you understand how to manage horses?" interrupted the Baron.

"Yes; I had the care of——"

"I mean," continued the Baron, cutting him short, "are you a good groom, and can you ride?"

"I was going to explain that my late master——" A knot rose in the poor fellow's throat, and stopped his speech.

"I did not ask you about your late master," said the Baron, peevishly.

"I beg your pardon," replied Carlino, abashed; "I meant to say that——in my last place I had the care of two horses, and they were as well groomed as any in Chambery."

"Very well, that is one point settled; you will have besides to keep my apartment in order, clean my boots: in short, perform all the duties of a servant."

"Yes, Monsieur le Baron; I know also how to cook."

"There's no occasion for that; I do not take my meals at home; only a cup of coffee in the morning, if you can make it. You can?—so much the better. The wages I give are a hundred francs a month, and you find yourself; will that do?"

"Perfectly, Monsieur le Baron."

"You bore me with your 'Monsieur le Baron;' 'Monsieur' is enough. Well then, be ready to start at seven this evening. Of course I take you on trial."

"I hope and trust that my zeal——"

"You are too talkative," interrupted the Baron. "Your late master, I am aware, allowed you more freedom than I am disposed to do. Keep this in mind —I hire you as my SERVANT" (the word doubly underlined). "And as to zeal—the less of it the better. Now you may go."

With this bucket of cold water on his head, Carlino made another low bow, and more bewildered than pleased, yet on the whole glad to have found a situation that took him to Paris, he went to announce his good fortune to Madame Ferrolliet, and to the household in general, and having received their congratulations, something reserved from those who knew the Baron best, hastened to pack up his clothes. His reflections while thus occupied were not entirely of a rosy hue. When he contrasted the harsh tones, the distant manner, the imperious ways of his new master, with the gentle voice, the gracious familiarity, the friendliness of his late one, his heart misgave him, and for the first time he feared that the life of a servant might not always be the realisation of that *beau-idéal* which up to this hour he had taken for granted it was.

Carlino, we may say, was born a servant, by which we mean that nature had intended and constituted him for one. All the instincts, energies, and bent of his being lay in that direction, and once having reached it, found full scope and satisfaction in that condition. He could conceive nothing within his range which he should prefer. To be dependent on some person in a position above his own, to have some one to please, to make comfortable, to look up to, to attach himself to, was a constitutional want with Carlino. Was his new master likely to satisfy this need? This was the question which in a rather confused shape now perplexed his mind and dimmed for a moment the lustre of his good-humoured smile. Only for a moment. Carlino was not the man to give way to despondency. His buoyancy and self-reliance —he had a large share of both—soon returned, and got the upper hand of his misgivings. He laid a wager with himself that, within a month, he would, by dint of care and attention, propitiate this gruff master of his.

Carlino was ready and under arms long before the specified hour. When the fatal moment of departure really came, the whole establishment, headed by Madame Ferrolliet, accompanied him as far as the *porte cochère*, and then followed endless kissings and shakings of hands, and good wishes, and recommendations to write, the whole interspersed with much weeping. Carlino, as he followed his master up the street, could scarcely see his way for blinding tears. The Baron, who had already taken his lofty farewell of the hostess, was, and looked, inexpressibly disgusted with all this fuss and sentimentality. At last it was over; but no—a new trial awaited master and servant at the coach-office. A group of the latter's acquaintances had assembled there to bid him farewell, and a new and augmented edition of kisses, handshakings, hopes, and what not, illustrated by sobs, and ohs! and ahs! was the consequence. Carlino was once more transformed into a fountain. The Baron could stand it no longer. To escape from the offensive scene, he took refuge in his corner of the *coupé*, from which he could not see what was passing without, nor, among other things, his servant, in spite of his heartache, running up the ladder leaning against the diligence, to make sure with his own eyes of the safety of his master's luggage. In a few minutes more Carlino installed himself in the *rotonde*, and the huge vehicle moved on towards Lyons. No railroad at that time existed between Lyons and Chambery.

At the first change of horses, Carlino, now quite himself again, got out, and stationed himself by his master's side of the *coupé*, within reach of his voice, whereupon the Frenchman, frowning ominously, turned his head the other way, with a pretence of not having seen him. This course of action was repeated and persevered in by both parties at every stage between Chambery and Lyons. The same at all the stoppages on the railroad from Lyons to Paris, with this trifling difference, that latterly Carlino stood in a pouring rain, and that his master no longer made a pretence of not seeing him, but actually did not see him, being comfortably fast asleep.

They reached Paris—the rain falling as fast as ever—at nine in the evening, and half-an-hour later were knocking at the *porte cochère* of the Baron's abode, Rue Madame. The *concierge*, light in hand, opened the door forthwith, and taking charge of the Baron's trunk (Carlino carried his own and his master's carpet bag), led the way to the first story, and proceeded to open a door. The Baron, turning to Carlino, said, "I do not want you to-night; the *concierge* will show you your room, and give you a light, and also a key of my apartment. Call me to-morrow morning at eight." This said, he entered the apartment.

The *concierge* led Carlino up three flights of stairs to his room, an attic, and there left him, as the Baron had ordered, with a lighted candle and a key of the apartment below, and the addition of a civil good-night.

The young man went at once to the bed, of which he stood in great want. Folding down the counterpane, he discovered there were no sheets; he had too often slept on hay to mind for one night the absence of the comfort of linen. He wound up his silver watch with great care, undressed in a twinkling, and in less time than it takes to write it was sleeping the sleep of the just.

CHAPTER II.

WITH the first dawn of day Carlino awoke as usual, got up, went to the window and opened it. A sea of roofs, bristling with chimneys innumerable, stretched before him as far as eye could reach. Now and then in the distance, emerging from the white September mist, rose towering over the rest a cupola, a spire, a column, like the gigantic mast of some leviathan ship. 'This then is Paris, thought he, and making a mock bow, he added, this time aloud, "Very glad to make your acquaintance, my dear sir." He was in capital spirits, and disposed, as you see, to be humorous; he was also very hungry, as hungry as a young man is likely to be who has tasted no food for the last twenty hours. The remedy was at hand, he drew from his trunk half of a big loaf, and a packet containing slices of sausage, and fell to *con amore*.

While munching his bread and sausage Carlino took a survey of his attic. The result was satisfactory. It was newly papered, and had an air both neat and gay: a bed, a capital iron one, two chairs, a small table on which were a waterless ewer and basin, and on the wall a wooden Nuremberg clock, constituted the whole of the furniture, plenty and to spare for a man of Carlino's habits. All the articles, bedding included, were not only new and clean, but free even from dust, which some provident hand must have lately removed. There was no fireplace, but our young valet was so little accustomed to one that he did not remark the hiatus. Lodged like a prince, thought he, and mounting on a chair he wound up the clock, setting it by his watch. This done, it was just half-past five, he locked his room door, and went down to his master's apartment.

Intent on not being heard, he turned the key in the lock with all the care of a thief, and entered on tiptoe a small lobby or ante-room, at the farther end of which were two doors at right angles; one was closed, the other ajar. Still using infinite caution, he pushed this last and found himself in a room of good dimensions, the destination of which as *salle à manger* was evidenced past all doubt by the heavy sideboards round it and the large oval table which stood in the centre. This *salle à manger* communicated by an inner door, happily at this moment wide open, with a passage leading, on one side to the kitchen, on the other to a good-sized sitting-room, longer than broad, a kind of study or library, hung with family pictures, below which, running all its length, were glazed bookcases. Between the two windows, placed in the breadth of the room, stood a huge something, and at the extremity *vis-à-vis* another huge something, both these mysterious objects carefully hid under a cover of green serge. Carlino, who was not a son of Eve for nothing, peeped under the serge, and discovered a collection of costly weapons, both ancient and modern, artistically arranged. The door at the farther end of this study being shut, Carlino thought it more prudent not to push his voyage of discovery any farther, for fear of perchance blundering into his master's room two hours too soon; so back he went to the kitchen.

Here an agreeable surprise awaited him; the first thing that caught his eye, protruding from the wall, just above the sink, was a cock, which, on being turned, gave forth an abundant supply of water. He had heard of dirty Auvergnats carrying up water to the apartments in Paris, and of so much being paid for every bucket of water, a practice he considered as both unnatural and degrading; therefore great was his relief at finding himself free from this double nuisance. He drank a good draught to help down the sausage, and improved the occasion to make his morning ablutions.

The kitchen was small, but airy and well lighted; the cooking utensils were *rari nantes* in it. One can see at a glance, thought he, with a melancholy shake of the head, that the master does not take his meals at home. In the course of his further investigations he came upon a heap of charcoal deposited under the stove, and found in a drawer a parcel of raw coffee, a machine for roasting it, and close by a coffee mill. In a moment he had lighted a fire, and to utilise the time the charcoal would take to be red-hot, he went to give air, sweep the dust, and set in order the rooms left at his disposal—a short and easy task, seeing that the apartment had evidently been taken good care of in the absence of the occupier. We forgot to say that he had found a broom behind the door of the kitchen, and plenty of dusters in a cupboard.

The rooms arranged, he returned to find his charcoal well ignited, so he roasted and ground some coffee, and set a jug of water all but boiling by the side of the fire. By the time all this was done it was scarcely half-past seven. Carlino was suddenly reminded of the trophies in the study by the sight of a piece of chamois leather, and he saw no reason why he should not employ the half hour still at his disposal in cleaning some of the costly weapons. Accordingly to the study he went, partly raised one of the serge covers, and took down the first articles within his reach, a brace of pistols, a cangiar, and a dagger, and set to work rubbing. At the first stroke of eight from a neighbouring clock he put aside his unfinished task, and knocking first at the closed door, entered what really proved to be the Baron's bedroom.

"Good-morning, sir, it is just striking eight," said Carlino. Monsieur gave a grunt. "I hope that Monsieur has passed a good night. Shall I open the blinds?" Another grunt. Carlino opened the blinds, and as he shut the window added, "As fine a day as ever a Christian could see." All these queries and remarks were against rules, and it was high time to check the fellow's familiarity. "Thank God, I have eyes of my own to see whether it is fine or not without being told," such was the gracious reply, in the most cantankerous of voices, which Carlino got for his pains. "Shall I bring the coffee?" asked he a little abashed. "Some warm water first; I will ring when I am ready for the coffee."

Baron Gaston was disposed to be more snappish

than usual. The fact is he felt a grudge against his new servant for having so soon recovered, and to all appearance so entirely, from the intemperate grief he had shown on leaving his Chambery friends. "The fellow has no heart," was the verdict passed on him by the Baron. And where is the wonder? Are machines expected to have hearts?

Monsieur had his warm water, rung for his coffee, and went to his study; Carlino, broom in hand, was just beginning to arrange the bedroom, when a furious pull at the bell made him rush into his master's presence. The Baron, in dressing-gown and slippers, was standing by the table, upon which lay the pistols, the cangiar, and the dagger. "Who gave you leave to touch these things?" asked he, with a look of Radamanthus.

"I beg your pardon," faltered Carlino, "I thought it was part of my duty——"

"You need never think," retorted the Baron; "I forbid you most positively ever to meddle with these arms, or so much as to look at them. I already told you I would have no zeal. Now go."

To have no zeal, forsooth! To exact that from Carlino was as much as to exact from the flame not to burn upwards, from the water not to run downwards. He was saturated with zeal, boiling over with zeal, made of zeal—zeal was the very essence of his being. The Baron's words cut the poor fellow to the quick. To be lowered to the level of an automaton, *who need not think*, and must only act when bidden— it was hard to bear, especially for a man who had been the right hand of his former master, and without whose advice not so much as a piece of furniture was displaced in that master's household. However, the first smart over, he bore the blow patiently—bore it because it was in his nature to be patient, and also because he knew his own worth, and was supported by the hope, nay, by the certainty, that his master would find it out in course of time, and end by coming round.

At half-past twelve Carlino was ordered to ask the *concierge* for the key of the stables, and to bring out the horse and groom it in the courtyard. The house was one *entre cour et jardin*, and the Baron, while dressing, could watch the proceeding from the window of the *cabinet de toilette* adjoining his bedroom. Presently he appeared down-stairs, hat and gloves on, and bidding Carlino have the horse saddled at two o'clock, went out. Carlino just ran up to the apartment, and locked the door, as he had been accustomed to do when no one was at home, and then returned to his grooming. At two precisely Monsieur was back, and in the saddle.

Carlino was struck dumb when he returned to the apartment to find the door wide open, and a man in shirt-sleeves, apparently quite at home, dancing in an odd sort of fashion up and down the dining-room. This person had a peculiar brush fastened to his right foot by a leather strap. "What are you doing?" asked Carlino.

"What am I doing?" repeated the intruder, "don't you see?—*Je frotte.*"

"How did you get in?" asked Carlino.

"Apparently through the door," answered the *frotteur* who seemed vastly diverted by the other's perplexed face.

"But I had locked the door," objected Carlino.

"And I unlocked it," rejoined the *frotteur*, never discontinuing his mysterious evolutions.

"Then you had a key?"

"Certainly—the *concierge* gave me his, as he always does when there is no one in the apartment."

Carlino went at once to the porter's lodge, and received full confirmation of the *frotteur's* statement. He made no remark, contenting himself with keeping a quiet eye upon the unknown functionary. Nevertheless, the proceeding seemed to him too irregular, and involving his personal responsibility too much, to be passed over without observation. Therefore, no sooner did the Baron return, than he felt it his duty to report the case. He said, "The *frotteur* has been here, sir."

"What if he has?" growled the Baron.

Carlino went on, "I had locked the door of the

apartment, while I finished grooming the horse, and he came in with the *concierge's* key."

"And what if he did?"

"Monsieur understands," went on Carlino, "that if strangers can come in at their pleasure——"

"I see what it is," interrupted the Baron, "two of a trade cannot agree."

"It is not that, sir, but—"

"I will have no squabblings—do you hear? Leave things as they are, and do not meddle with what is no business of yours, or we shall part before long."

Carlino would have persisted, but his master went in, banging the door after him.

Not many minutes after, the ringing of the study bell summoned him again to his master's presence. "I am going out; you are free to do what you please till ten o'clock. If I am not home by that time, leave a lighted lamp in the ante-room, and go to bed." Having said this, the Baron again went out.

It was then nearly six o'clock. By seven Carlino, having finished all he had to do in the house and in the stables, went to a neighbouring small restaurant, and had a dish of meat and potatoes with bread *ad libitum*. He was a great bread eater, but abstemious as to wine. His hunger appeased, he took a stroll in the garden of the Luxembourg close by. Long before nine he was at home again; he lighted a candle, and read a few pages of "Le Novelle del Soave"—a gift from the defunct prefect. This book constituted all Carlino's library — he never tired of reading it again and again, nor of falling asleep over its leaves, as was now actually the case. The striking of ten o'clock roused him from his pleasant doze, and at once he lighted a lamp and placed it in the anteroom. Having obeyed implicitly the one-half of his orders, why not the other?—because zeal, that terrible enemy of his, whispered in his ear that he had better sit up a little longer. He yielded to the prompting, and fell profoundly asleep.

The grating of the key in the lock startled him out of his slumbers. "What are you doing here?" asked the Baron sternly.

"I beg pardon. I thought Monsieur might perhaps want me."

"I told you once before you were not to think, but to do as you were bid. Let me catch you again here after ten o'clock, and you are discharged." These last words were pronounced in such a tone as to leave a deep impression on Carlino's mind that they conveyed no empty threat. In silence he took up his candle, and went to his attic, saying to himself, "What a bear of a master I have chanced on!"

Days and weeks passed by, and the glacier showed no signs of thawing—in other words, there was no coaxing or forcing M. le Baron, even for a moment, out of his distant manner and uncommunicative ways.

Every attempt on Carlino's part to trespass beyond the magic circle of his strictly official business was as resolutely repulsed, and as sharply resented as on the first day. One morning among others (to quote a last instance of the ferocious jealousy with which this gentleman guarded from any infringement what we suppose he considered his dignity), one morning Carlino had had a beautiful dahlia given to him, we will say by whom by-and-by. Among the gimcracks scattered on a table in the study, which at that moment he was dusting, he had often noticed a small vase, in the shape of a lotus, seemingly destined to hold flowers; and it occurred to him that his dahlia would just suit it. So he half filled the vase with water, and placed the dahlia in it. An hour or so after, Monsieur went into the study. A tremendous ring at the bell brought Carlino running to the study. "Who put that flower there?" asked Monsieur, in his iciest tone. "I did," said Carlino, more smiling than ever. "Then remove it this instant," was the retort, "and take no such liberty in future. When I want flowers, I know where to buy them."

Hating such occasional rebuffs, and the smart attaching to the denial of all fellow-feeling which they implied, Carlino had in other respects nothing to complain of, and much to be thankful for in his new situation. To begin with, his master, if not kind, which he certainly was not, neither was he unkind; if he never praised, neither did he ever find fault, so long as not intruded on. And in a man so rigidly undemonstrative as was the Baron, this negative mood might be interpreted as a tacit acknowledgment of the goodness of the service, and of his satisfaction with it. For, it need scarcely be said, with a person of Carlino's experience and good-will, the service went on like clock-work. This result, we must add, was greatly helped by the Baron's methodical habits and even tenour of life, high merits in Carlino's eyes, and indeed in those of all really good servants, and for which he was truly grateful. Then, the situation in itself could scarcely have been better. There was certainly plenty to do, both in the apartment and in the stables, but not more than an active young man could manage without being overworked. Then he was his own master from six to ten. His wages were considerable, far more than what he had had from the late prefect; and he had calculated that with his sober habits he might, without pinching himself, save fifty francs a month, lay by twenty-four pounds a year. Quite a treasure! He could accomplish this the more easily as he had found, to his grateful surprise, that his master paid for his washing, though this item had not been mentioned in their verbal agreement.

With Carlino's character, it was a mere matter of course that he should be on the best terms with the *concierge* and his wife, as with all the other servants in the house. Indeed, who could help being pleased with his cheerful, honest face, and obliging ways? Last, not least, he had made a friend, found a confidante, in the giver of the dahlia, Mademoiselle Victorine, his neighbour in the attic, the lady's maid and *souffre douleur* of the Marchioness of the second floor. Mademoiselle Victorine was not a favourable specimen of a Parisian *soubrette;* she was small, red-haired (red hair was not yet the fashion at that epoch), much freckled, and without being positively a humpback, made you think of one. Her mistress was not ashamed (at least the scandalous chronicle was positive on this point) to take advantage of these physical imperfections, serious impediments to the girl's finding a good place, to treat her as a slave, pay her very small wages, and literally starve her. Victorine had an old mother, whom she managed out of her small earnings to keep from dying, and for the sake of that mother suffered uncomplainingly, nay, cheerfully. This acquaintance, which soon ripened into a real friendship, was precious to Carlino in many ways. It opened a safety-valve to his pent-up communicativeness, satisfied in a reasonable degree his cravings for sympathy, and by a natural comparison of Victorine's lot with his, reconciled him with his own. Contrasting it with that of this poor drudge, who was poorly paid, under-fed, systematically scolded and ridiculed, obliged to wait up till her worldly mistress came home at two and three in the morning—contrasting, we repeat, his life and hers, Carlino might consider himself a spoilt child of fortune. Carlino felt for her, paid her all the little attentions in his power, cheered her when despondent, took her whenever she was free, not often the case, for a walk in the garden of the Luxembourg, or to the quays to see the shops, and admire the engravings there exposed for sale, for Victorine had a taste for art.

Of love-making between them there could be no question. Victorine, setting aside her personal defects, might have been his mother; and it was the tone of a mother, or of an elder sister, affectionate with a little infusion of superior wisdom, that she had adopted, and never wavered from, with him. Carlino rarely went out only for a walk, especially since the days were short; his dinner at the wine-shop once over, he went up to his garret, and employed himself, either mending his clothes—he was a capital hand at the needle—or in playing on an instrument, resembling a brass comb, some one or other of his national airs. In this poor pocket harmonica consisted all the poetry of Carlino's existence. It evoked the vine-clad hills of his Piedmontese birth-place, it brought before him the familiar faces of father and mother long since gone to their rest, it reminded him of the joys and trials of his boyhood. It had stood by him like a faithful friend from his earliest years, and had soothed many a bitter pang. It was the muse of his melancholy hours, neither many nor of long duration. Once the tiny instrument was replaced in its case, and the moisture rubbed from his eyes, Carlino was himself again, that is to say, the buoyant, hopeful, warm-hearted creature nature had meant him to be.

The only person within the circle of Carlino's acquaintance, his relations with whom left much to be desired in point of cordiality, was the *frotteur*. This last, a true son of Paris, was caustic and much given to quizzing; whereas the former, a true Piedmontese, was slow of repartee, and, like many greater men, unable to enjoy a joke at his own expense. So there was no love lost between them. Carlino looked upon the *frotteur* as a nuisance and an intruder, and the *frotteur* on his side divined anything but a well-wisher in the Italian. The hebdomadal visit of this functionary was a thorn in Carlino's flesh. He felt it to be not only provoking, but degrading, to have to wait the pleasure of this floor-rubber in order to give the last finishing touches to *his* apartment. Was it not alike the duty and the right of a good servant to do *all* that had to be done in the apartment confided to his care? Then Zeal, that irrepressible Zeal, which could not be kept down, again whispered in his ear that to pay this jackanapes fifteen francs a month for what he, Carlino, could and would do for nothing, was throwing money out of the window.

Actuated by these feelings, Carlino determined to learn how to frotter—a very easily acquired talent—and thus dispense with the services of this interloper. To this end he carefully watched the various phases of the frotteing process, and once having mastered them, bought the various necessary implements, and began, when alone, practising the art on his own account. This, however, could not be done for any time without leaving traces, which in the long-run did not escape, any more than their drift, the experienced eye of the *frotteur en titre*. Thereupon the threatened functionary lost not a moment in complaining to Carlino's master, alleging that the Piedmontese, with his clumsy attempts to *frotter*, spoiled the *parquet*. The Baron, much against the grain, demanded an explanation of his servant. Carlino gave it, and candidly admitted that he had practised frotteing with a view to exercising the *frotteur's* functions himself, and indignantly repelled the charge of injuring the floor.

The Baron, who had listened with undisguised impatience to Carlino's prolix statement, said, "The short and the long of it is, you want to pocket the fifteen francs a month."

"God forbid," protested Carlino; "what I wanted was to save Monsieur the unnecessary outlay of a hundred and eighty francs a year."

Carlino was really appalled by the fearful and sudden change in his master's countenance. The

Baron grew purple, and his eyes burned like carbuncles.

"Impudent boor!" cried he in a terrible passion; "who gave you leave to economize for me?" Carlino, terrified out of his wits, would have explained, but in vain. "Leave the room!" thundered his master, rising with a threatening gesture; "leave the room, or by all the saints . . . . !"

What could be at the root of this sudden violence? Simply this, that the Baron was far from rich—indeed, for a man of his rank and tastes, he was positively poor, and ashamed of being poor. His ticklishness on this point amounted almost to mania. Any, even the most covert, hint at his straitened circumstances from an equal, he would have resented as an insult, which nothing but blood could wash away; coming from a menial, and as such beneath his vengeance, he felt it as a disgrace past help, "le coup de pied de l'âne," as a Frenchman would say. Why he did not at once dismiss the offender, remains a mystery. Carlino, who had never seen him in such a fury, expected his discharge; and, indeed, little cared if he did receive it, so disgusted was he with the Baron's ungraciousness. But having vented his spleen to his neighbour and confidante in the attic, her sympathy healed this wound also. Carlino was the last man to bear anybody malice, and least of all to the master whose bread he ate. A week had scarcely gone by, when he had quite recovered his equanimity and his look of contentment. Not so Monsieur, whose mien and voice, whenever he spoke to Carlino, betrayed from this day a concentrated feeling of irritation.

November arrived, bringing along with it more than its ordinary train of mist, cold, and rain. One day Monsieur, who still went out riding, only at a much earlier hour than before, was caught in a heavy shower, and returned home wet to the skin. The consequence was a cold which, strong as a horse as he was, and still more self-willed, the Baron made light of. Though feeling far from well, and coughing a good deal, he rode as usual, went out in all weathers as usual, smoked as usual, as though bent on conquering by main force his indisposition. It proved, however, stronger than his will, as evinced by the fact that a day came—it was the fourth since his wetting—when he felt unequal to going out. He had a large fire in the study, with a kettle of boiling water by its side, and spent all the day there wrapped in his dressing-gown. Carlino would have made him some *tisane*, or prepared some *bouillon*, or vermicelli, or tapioca soup, but all these proposals met with a peremptory and ungracious "No." The Baron, like most old bachelors, had a system of his own for all ailments—no food, and strong, hot grog. Seeing that he was not better on the morrow, on the contrary, that the fits of coughing were more frequent and violent, Carlino timidly ventured to suggest the expediency of sending for a doctor, a hint which was answered by "Don't bother me."

This was not to be the last of Carlino's indiscretions during that day. The Baron was worse towards evening and went to bed—his breathing was short and hoarse, his cough unceasing. Carlino felt uneasy, and great was his perplexity as ten o'clock approached. Was he, according to orders, to leave the Baron alone and helpless, in case he should grow worse, or was he to remain at hand, at the risk of perhaps being discharged? The balance was sure to incline to the side of zeal. Carlino tried to convince himself, and succeeded in doing so, that there was no chance of Monsieur, ill as he was, getting up to wander about the apartment. On the strength of this conviction, Carlino took off his shoes, and with a beating heart sat down on a chair in the study, and listened. The study, as we know, was contiguous to the Baron's bedchamber, and the least sound in the one room, were it nothing but a sigh, could be heard in the other.

For a good couple of hours the Baron's incessant cough kept Carlino wide awake; but then there came a lull, and exhausted nature began to assert its rights. Carlino's eyelids grew first heavy, then closed, and sleep stole over him. Now a man sleeping in an awkward and inconvenient position, though not an habitual snorer, is apt to emit now and then guttural or nasal sounds of considerable intensity. Such was just the case with Carlino, who, after a series of moderate snorts, was betrayed into one so much louder than the rest, that he awoke himself with the sound. He listened for awhile—complete silence prevailed, and he resolved on a speedy retreat. He rose from his chair with the greatest precaution, and groped for his shoes; he had just caught hold of them, when the door of communication opened, and the Baron, candle in hand, appeared on the threshold.

"Dogging me, are you?" said the gentleman, icily. "I suspected as much—I will have no spies about me. You are discharged."

Had the Baron struck him Carlino would not have resented it half so much as he did the name of spy. Carlino, be it remembered, came from a country enslaved for ages, and where the trade of spy had flourished and was still flourishing, to the disgust and abhorrence of all honest-hearted people. The greatest insult which could be offered an Italian was to call him a spy. No wonder, then, that, humble and submissive as he was, Carlino winced and smarted under the infliction, just as a quiet, well-broken horse will do when the lash falls upon a sore place.

He said with some dignity: "I have sinned against Monsieur's orders, and Monsieur has a right to dismiss me, if he please; but Monsieur has no right to call me a spy."

"Indeed," sneered the Baron.

"Yes, indeed," continued Carlino, warmly; "my late master was a first-rate Liberal; he knew me from my boyhood, and would not have given his confidence to a spy."

"What is the man raving about?" said the Baron, in unaffected surprise.

"I am not raving, but speaking the plain truth," replied Carlino. "Write to the Syndic of Bovino, my native place, and see if I am not telling the truth."

The Baron, who had no clue to his servant's peculiar train of thought, and consequent emotion, shrugged his shoulders and turned to go.

"Monsieur must be so good as to listen to me for another moment. I was not spying, I was giving Monsieur a proof of attachment . . . ."

"Keep your attachment to yourself," retorted the Baron; "I don't want it."

"I know you don't, and the more's the pity," went on Carlino; "for permit me to tell you that you will never be well served except by an attached servant, and you will never have such a one unless you show that you value him. A man, though he is a servant, is not the less a man, with a man's feelings. You have some affection for your horse, you pat him on the neck, you encourage him with kind words when he is good. Why should you do less for a Christian who has a soul to be saved, just as you have?"

The bedroom door closed on these last words. Carlino picked up his shoes, and went up to his attic and to bed, where for the first time he slept but little, so heavily did the word spy weigh upon his mind. For the first time, also, Carlino's bright smile was absent when he went the next morning, according to custom, to call Monsieur at eight o'clock.

"You have eight days to look for another situation," said Monsieur.

"Thank you," replied Carlino; "but I do not mean to seek for another here; I shall go back to my country."

"In that case," said the Baron, "I shall pay your journey."

"Monsieur is very good," said Carlino.

"I shall need some days to provide myself with a servant," added the Baron.

"As many as Monsieur pleases," assented Carlino. There was nothing either aggressive or conciliatory in the Baron's voice or manner—both were those of complete indifference.

Carlino, after serious reflection, had come to the conclusion that it would be better for him to give up strange lands and to seek for employment in his own country. His personal experience, aided by that of

Mdlle. Victorine, had gone far to create in his mind a strong prejudice against French masters and mistresses, while his recollection of the prefect disposed him to invest the fellow-countrymen of that master and benefactor with the possession of all the best qualities. As to Paris, his stay had been too short to allow of his liking it enough to leave it with regret—he was glad to have seen it for the sake of being able to say that he had done so; but the huge metropolis, with its incessant noises, and rush of people and carriages, bewildered rather than attracted him. His only regret was for Mdlle. Victorine, that unfortunate creature who stood so much in need of a friend and comforter, and who was going to lose him, her sole comforter and friend.

The Baron was so much better as to be able to go out in the afternoon, but came home early and went to bed early. Five days passed as smooth as oil; strange faces came and remained closeted with Monsieur le Baron. On the afternoon of the sixth day, he said to Carlino, "You are at liberty to go, I have provided myself with a servant."

"I will leave to-morrow morning, if that suit Monsieur."

Carlino spent his leisure hours of that day, from six to ten, in thoroughly cleaning the kitchen, putting his things together, and in treating Mdlle. Victorine to a walk—her last walk with him. It was a very sad one, and Mdlle. Victorine returned from it nearly heart-broken.

Carlino rose on the following morning, as was his wont, with the dawn—he had not had a wink of sleep, poor fellow! He arranged his room with the utmost nicety, and then made his way down-stairs. The door of the apartment on the second story was ajar. Mdlle. Victorine was lying in wait behind it. As Carlino was passing, she pushed it open, seized both his hands, and pressing something into one of them, said between one sob and another—"Keep this in remembrance of me. I dare not stop longer—Good-bye, and a good journey. God bless you, Carlino!"

"Thank you," said Carlino, also much moved; "I shall keep your present as a sacred relic till the last day of my life. God bless you also!" and so saying, he drew her close to him, and kissed her on each cheek, and then on the mouth, Italian fashion. Victorine's *souvenir* to Carlino was a silk purse, white, red, and green—the Italian colours—a work of patient affection, with which she had beguiled many a long hour of the night while sitting up for her mistress. Carlino folded up Victorine's keepsake in a sheet of clean paper, and put it in his pocket; then performed his customary work, lighted the fire, swept and dusted the rooms, that he might leave everything in order. As eight o'clock struck, he was just going to carry a jug of warm water to his master, when the door opened, and in came a tall black whiskered man, who asked whether the Baron was up.

"Are you the new servant?" inquired Carlino. The stranger answered that he was. "Well, take in the warm water, and tell your master that I am waiting his pleasure." The man returned presently, and said that the Baron would see Carlino by and by. Carlino ran up to his attic, brought down his trunk to the lodge, and begged the porter to fetch him a *citadine* at nine precisely. A good half hour after he had gone upstairs again, the new servant brought him word that the Baron was at liberty to see him in the study.

Carlino, first knocking at the door, went in, and at sight of Monsieur seated as usual by the fire with a small desk before him; combined with the thought that he saw him for the last time, a lump rose in his throat, and he would have given something to have indulged in a good fit of crying; but he made an effort and adjourned that relief to the next moment of leisure. "Here are the keys of the apartment, Monsieur," said Carlino, steadying his voice as well as he could. "If I have offended Monsieur in word or deed, I hope Monsieur will believe that I erred through ignorance, and from no want of good-will or respect, and I humbly beg Monsieur's pardon. I wish Monsieur good health, and all manner of happiness."

"Thank you," replied Monsieur. "I give you credit for having intended well. Here," handing Carlino some money, "are your wages for the present month—the rest for your journey. See if it is right."

"I have no doubt it is, sir," said Carlino, putting the money in his pocket.

"Well, then, good-bye. I wish you success in your own country."

"Many thanks to Monsieur," said Carlino, and, with a low obeisance, left the room.

His successor was waiting for him in the *salle à manger*, and said to him, "So you are off."

"Yes, I am," was Carlino's answer.

"Between us, is the place a good one?" asked the other, with a knowing wink.

"Excellent," said Carlino.

"Why then leave?"

"Because the air of Paris is bad for my chest. Good-day."

As he crossed the court on his way to the lodge, Carlino turned round and saw Victorine all in tears at a window of the second story. She motioned to him with her handkerchief, and he waved his hand to her in return. This last farewell nearly brought about a crisis; all the pent-up emotions of the last twenty-four hours made a rush in search of an outlet, and it was in a most pitiable state that the poor young man took leave of the porter and his wife. At last he was in the *citadine* alone, and at liberty to keep the promise he had made to himself of a good cry. And he kept his promise so completely that the coachman had some difficulty in wrenching from him the explanation that he was to drive to the Lyons terminus.

Que voulez-vous? these lumps of flesh for hire, as Baron Gaston graphically defined servants—these nobodies will have feelings and cry their eyes out, and be miserable to their hearts' content, just as much as though they were somebodies. It is not to be borne.

CHAPTER III.

IT would be an exaggeration to say that Baron Gaston was touched or somewhat deeply impressed by the mixture of humility and dignity with which Carlino had taken leave of him. We shall be nearer the truth if we simply state that the Baron had felt and noted the difference of his late servant's exit from that of his predecessors, a difference all to the advantage of the latter. Perhaps during the first month or so after Carlino's departure the Baron might have thought once or twice, *à propos* of some clumsiness or slowness of the servant *in esse*, how much more quickly and cleverly Carlino would have managed; but that was all. At the end of a couple of months he had slipped as entirely from the Baron's memory as if he had never been in his service; even his name, odd sounding though it was to French ears, was forgotten.

The Baron's mode of life had in nothing varied; he rode a good deal as usual, and changed his servants every second month as usual, kept to his unsociable habits, saw very few people, and guarded his dignity from intrusion as jealously as ever. The evenness of his life, however, was unexpectedly interrupted by the sudden death of his uncle, the Vidame, in the month of August, 1854. Just as the Baron was preparing for his yearly visit to the Castle, he received a telegram from Chambery, to announce that his old relative had had an apoplectic stroke, and was not expected to survive.

The Baron started immediately, but to no purpose. When he reached the Castle the Vidame was dead. He arrived in time, however, to have the corpse exposed in a *chapelle ardente*, open to the public, where it lay in state for a day and night. All the neighbourhood, of course, flocked to see it. At the expiration of the four-and-twenty hours the body was put into a costly coffin; conveyed to Chambery, and, after a princely funeral, consigned to earth in the cemetery of Chambery. It had been the express desire of the Vidame, repeatedly manifested during his life to his nephew, and moreover stated in his will, that his bones should rest in the country of his adoption, where he had spent the best part of his life.

After the funeral the deceased's will was opened, and, according to general expectation, the Baron was left sole legatee, with merely the onus of paying a certain yearly pension during their lives to two or three of the testator's old servants. The inheritance, though not magnificent, was not to be disdained. It consisted of the Castle, and of the extensive vineyard adjoining, the produce of which was held in high esteem, and always commanded high prices. The heir found also among his uncle's papers, as much to his astonishment as to his pleasure, a rather large number of titles of stock in the Piedmontese funds—of that very State whose downfall he had never tired of hoping and predicting for the last four or five years.

Baron Gaston was detained at the Castle much longer than he could have wished—first, by the gathering of the grapes, which that year proved uncommonly plentiful, and yielded excellent wine; and secondly, by business connected with the inheritance, obliging him frequently to communicate with his late uncle's notary, residing in Chambery. And, as a natural consequence, whenever he went thither he put up as before at the Hôtel de l'Europe. On one of these occasions Madame Ferrolliet mentioned Carlino, and the Baron had the double condescension to explain that he had parted with the man on account of his excessive familiarity, and to inquire what had become of the fellow. Madame Ferrolliet replied that Carlino had been employed all the summer at the Baths of Acqui, but she could not say in what capacity. She had had this news from a commercial traveller, a countryman of Carlino's. Eleven months had passed since the Baron and Carlino had parted.

We have said nothing of the Baron's grief for the loss of his old relation, because, if he felt any sorrow, it may be considered of the nature of the imponderables. Not for the world would the Baron have neglected to pay his yearly allegiance to the chief of the family, not for the world would he have allowed a word less than respectful to the Vidame to pass without calling the offender to account; but, as we have already said, at the root of all this attention and touchiness there lay nothing but pride, family pride; of real affection there was little or none. The Baron's sentiments towards his uncle were somewhat akin to those of certain husbands towards their better halves, for whom they care very moderately, but for whose honour, in so far as reflecting their own, they are very ticklish.

It was not till the month of December that the Baron returned to Paris, and resumed his habitual occupations. His income was nearly doubled, and without being rich, at least according to his ideas, he was very well off. He made no change, however, in his simple style of living—he liked simplicity for its own sake,—he made no change, save one, he gave himself the luxury of a second horse; four months of active life in the country, the greater part of the time spent in the open air, had given him a renewed lease of youth. No one would have guessed him to be forty-five, and all his acquaintances—friends he had none—congratulated him on his good looks. He had not for years felt so strong and hale, or been in such excellent spirits. Under such happy auspices opened the new year of 1855 for him, that year which fate had marked for his destruction. Thus we see a gallant ship, manned by a gallant crew, set sail with a fair wind under a glorious sky, to be shortly miserably wrecked on some unknown sunken rock.

Our Baron was born with a passion for horses, which had been perhaps his chief inducement to entering a cavalry regiment. Indulgence had strengthened instead of weakening this passion; and we have seen him, on his return to the life of a civilian, pinching himself sorely in order to be able to keep a horse, become a necessity of life for him. His skill in the management of a stable was on a par with his predilection for it; and his opinion as to horses had a certain authority in the sporting world. Adepts gave him credit for being a first-rate rider, only too daring, and prognosticated that some day or other he would come to grief. In fact he courted difficulty and danger, and many were the animals, pronounced unmanageable, that he had broken into obedience. Among the members of the club frequented by Baron de Kerdiat was a rich young Count, just of age. This young man had bought a beautiful bay mare, and discovered too late that she was a vicious, shying beast, far too much for him. Some mutual acquaintance advised him to apply to the Baron, and so he did. The Baron, after examination of the mare, gave it as his opinion that the case was not a hopeless one, and offered to take her in hand.

All bid fair in the beginning to justify the opinion he had given. Under his management the mare improved rapidly and steadily. But there came a day when she proved as fractious as though he had never mounted her. It was in one of the avenues of the Bois de Boulogne that her rebellion began in earnest, followed by one of the most terrible struggles on record between man and beast,—we might rather term it a deadly duel. The mare went quietly enough a certain distance, till she came in front of a large tree, but once there, neither persuasion nor compulsion could make her pass it. The Baron tried long and patiently all the methods and manœuvres calculated to overcome her resistance, but all to no purpose. Meanwhile all the riders in the Bois had flocked to the spot, and so had also a crowd of pedestrians. This was the Baron's ruin. His fame was at stake, and self-love urged him to rush to a conclusion, that is, to obtain by main force what alone might possibly have been obtained by time and patience from the animal's exhaustion.

He turned back some hundred paces, and then again approached the tree at a gentle canter—then, when close to the critical point, he tightened the curb, dug his spurs into her sides, and struck her sharply between the ears. All this was done simultaneously. The anxiety of the onlookers was so intense that not a creature stirred or spoke. In an instant the maddened animal was on her hind legs spinning round and round, and then with a monstrous bound forwards threw her rider out of the saddle. The Baron's ponderous body was dashed against the trunk of the tree, the unconscious occasion of the disaster. A cry of horror broke from the bystanders. The unfortunate man was picked up, to all appearance, dead, put into a carriage, together with a physician who volunteered his services, and conveyed home. During the evening the news of the accident spread from club to club, and the next day a paragraph appeared in all the morning papers, stating that the Baron had been thrown by the Count's mare, and killed on the spot.

The rumour was false. The Baron was not dead.

The Baron was spared to wish—oh, how often!—that he were so. In that prostrate form, as white and stiff as death, there yet lurked a spark of life, which nature and science combined succeeded in fanning into a flame again. It was found that the external hurts were not of consequence, but the internal ones were most serious. The spine was so injured as to produce paralysis, complete as to the lower limbs, partial as to the upper, attended by fits of excruciating pain.'

The patient did not begin to realise his situation until he was allowed to leave his bed for a sofa. He refused to be carried thither, as the doctor had recommended, and insisted on walking to it. Vain attempt! His legs gave way under him as though they had been of water. They had lost all power and sensibility. This was three weeks after the accident. One more week, and he was allowed to leave the sofa for an easy chair. Again he refused to be carried, and supported by a thick stick he endeavoured to walk the five paces. Just as impossible as to make the tour of the globe. Still he hoped against hope—hoped impossible things—to be able some day, when he was stronger in health, to collect all his energies in a supreme effort at standing, and work a miracle on himself—to wake some morning after a good night's rest and find the stiffness and numbness of his legs all gone.

Days and weeks and months passed, and no miracle

occurred, and his helplessness continued the same. Thus, sip by sip, as it were, he imbibed the consciousness of his all but desperate condition. Yet he did not despair. Why should he? Where nature alone failed, nature aided by art would and should succeed. What else were physicians for, if not for helping nature? One after another he called in all the luminaries of the Paris Faculty, and told them, "I must and will be cured;—is it not possible?" The luminaries, one and all, declared that it was, that they had seen cases as serious as his perfectly cured, assured him of the unlimited resources of nature and art, spoke of the wonderful recoveries effected by the waters of Ems, by hydropathy, by the climate of Algeria; but one and all warned him of the dangers of locomotion for the present. The shock to the nervous centres was yet too recent to allow of his venturing even upon a short journey. It is in no spirit of disparagement that we record the inconclusive suggestions of the Faculty—they were dictated by humanity. Could they tell the sufferer that they considered his case hopeless, as they did? Could they send him on a useless journey, at a too probable risk of accelerating a final crisis?

"But in the meanwhile," urged the Baron, "am I to remain in this horrible condition, doing nothing?"

The physicians said that he might try Barège baths, steam baths, electricity, moxa. The natural bent of the Baron was towards kill or cure remedies. He began by moxas, with no other result than of making a martyr of himself; he then had resort to electricity, then to Bains de Barège—nothing availed.

Day after day, week after week, month after month, beheld him forced to lie for hours and hours together stretched on his sofa, or propped up in his arm-chair, his imperious will imprisoned in a case of lead, another Prometheus riven to his rock, devouring in silence his tears of anguish and rage. His only support in this cruellest of trials was the consciousness that nevertheless he was still the master of his own destiny. There yet remained in his benumbed arms and hands power of motion and sense of touch sufficient to enable him to cock a pistol, and .... have done with it.

Marks of sympathy and interest he did not lack. In the first place, all the sporting world made a point of leaving their cards at his door, and as soon as he could receive visits, the members of his club, old comrades, casual acquaintances called upon him, and helped to beguile some of the heavy hours. Each and all had words of comfort and encouragement, each and all had their peculiar panacea for his malady. The cousin of this one, who had been in a worse plight than the Baron, had been cured by hydropathy; this other, who had been a cripple for eleven months, owed his recovery to Aix-les-Bains; another had witnessed a marvellous restoration effected in an analogous case by homœopathy; another by a stay of five weeks on the Righi. They laughed at his fears that he was a cripple for life, and all this, in spite of his disbelief in the efficacy of their suggestions, did him good. Hydropathy alone, being, as it is, a violent process, had an attraction for him.

But as time elapsed, and there came no change for the better, the bulk of visitors began to thin, and the visits of the few who remained faithful grew rare and far between. During the second month, even the faithful ones had begun to fail in their attentions, and by the end of the third, the poor sick man was most of the day alone. Paris, with its great distances and its numerous diversions, is a terrible dissolvent of active sympathies. The Baron, as we have said, had no friends—only acquaintances, and these soon weary, especially of a morose and often ill-humoured invalid. He had sown indifference, and he reaped isolation. Not altogether though.

One hand, one heart had offered themselves to him in his great need, and he had cast them aside. Three weeks or so after his fall he had received a letter worded thus:

"Only a week ago I learned by the public papers, with what feelings you may better imagine than I describe, the terrible accident which has befallen you.

Thank God! things are not so bad as, in their precipitation, the journals stated them to be. From the same source I gather that you are still in bed, and that your convalescence is likely to be long, and to demand great care. An estrangement of eight years, not of my doing, has not altered my sentiments nor cooled my heart towards you. Say only one word, and in a few hours you will have by your side

"Your devoted and affectionate sister,

"MARIE MORON *née* DE KERDIAT.

" LE MANS, *February 1st.*

"P.S.—My husband knows and approves of what I write."

A short but sharp struggle of feelings succeeded the perusal of this letter. The offer was tempting. He knew that the writer would be true to her word. He hesitated, but pride carried the day. He crumpled up the letter, and threw it into the waste-paper basket. Such was all the answer it received.

Marie Moron, the Baron's younger sister—younger by sixteen years—had been guilty of a *mésalliance*, an unpardonable sin in her brother's eyes and in those of their uncle, the Vidame, and for which both of them had disowned her, and had broken off all communication with her from that time to this. She had married for love a man whose mind and heart would have adorned even the most exalted station in life, but who could not show—what he little cared for—the least shred of a pedigree, and who possessed nothing in the world but what he earned by the sweat of his brow in the capacity of schoolmaster in a provincial town; in short, according to the Baron's theory, a nobody.

The Baron's infirmity necessitated some alterations in the economy of his household. First, he had to part with his horses, a sacrifice which cost him a bitter pang. Setting apart his affection for his grandmother, horses had been the sole preference of his life, and to renounce them was to renounce the joy of his existence. Then he had to engage a woman as cook, and the man-servant had to leave the room in the attic, and sleep in Monsieur's *cabinet de toilette*, to be ready for any emergency. Nor were these external changes the only ones entailed by his malady. So long as he had had visitors during the greater part of the day, to give assistance and help him in a thousand ways, he had remained as stiff and uncommunicative as of old to his servants. But when visits became rare and far between, when he had no one to depend upon to minister to his hourly wants but his servants, and was necessarily in constant communication with them, his haughty and taciturn habits gradually and involuntarily relaxed. Nay, there came a day—say, after a week, as it were, of solitary confinement—

when he would have begged as a favour from the one or the other, had not pride and false shame barred the way,—when he would have begged his servants to sit down by him and gossip, only that he might hear human voices, and so make sure that he was not yet in his tomb. Nay, more than that, there came a day when he doubted the soundness of his life-long system of dealing with those who served him, and thought to himself, after perhaps ringing half-a-dozen times in vain, what a comfort it would be now to him to have made a friend of a servant, at the cost of a little familiarity and kindness.

By a natural transition, he thought of Carlino, contrasting his service with that of the mercenary creatures he had now about him; he remembered Carlino's continued good-will, which he had considered necessary to check; he recalled the poor fellow's good-natured smile, which had so grated on his nerves, blind as he was! What a godsend it would be to have the Piedmontese back again! How those words of Carlino's kept sounding in his ears, "You will never be well served but by an attached servant, and you will never secure such a one unless you repay him in kind!" With what regretful longing did he now think of Carlino, Carlino whom he had sent away so harshly, for what? for a proof of attachment. Which of his present servants would voluntarily sit up during a night for him because he had a cold? And for that he had dismissed him, scorning to his face that attachment—fool that he had been!

Thus the force of circumstances led our haughty Baron, led him by insensible degrees, to feel, and acknowledge, and bow to that law of mutual dependence of man on man, however different their station, for which the French have a phrase so admirably expressive, *Solidarité Humaine*, that most English first-rate writers have of late adopted it, slightly Anglicised. We only sketch the phases through which the Baron's mind passed—it would be too long and too dreary work to describe the transitions which linked these phases together.

The Baron's involuntary exigencies were so great and so many that only a sincere devotion could have met them. A baby is not more helpless than he was, he could do nothing for himself—to rise, to dress, to get to bed, even to change a posture on his sofa, when in pain, required a helping hand. His present servants were neither better nor worse than the generality of their kind, but they were not certainly devoted. Why should they have been so? He was a perfect stranger to them, and little amiable by nature, his actual awful sufferings were not calculated to render him so now. He paid handsome wages, it is true, but he gave a great deal of trouble, and the servants considered their wages scarcely a sufficient compensation for the extra work required. Then the house was so dull, either silent as a tomb, or resounding with sighs and groans when the master had his fits of pain, which but too frequently occurred. No wonder that they wanted some relaxation; no wonder that the cook, when she went out to make purchases, should by way of diversion chatter rather freely and lengthily with the portress, the grocer, and the butcher; no wonder that the man-servant, when sent on an errand, should resort in the first place to the wine-shop round the corner, to vent his spleen over a bottle, and to relate to the other servants he met there the life of a dog his master led him. Meanwhile that master might ring the bell and shout as much as he pleased, the only answer he got was the echo of his own voice.

A man of action and not of thought, the Baron was without arms against his *ennui*. Reading, that great comforter and soother of invalids, had never been a resource to him, rather a bore—and so it proved even now. He took in the daily newspapers, the reviews, the newest novel, but found little relief from them. He was too full of himself, and of his own great misery to sympathise with fictitious personages and mishaps, which were to his what a molehill is to Mont Blanc. Nor did he take any interest in politics, which seemed to him a stale, unprofitable concern. What did he care about the Eastern, or

Italian, or Polish question? The question of all questions for him was to get cured.

His favourite pastime was to have his arm-chair rolled to the window of the dining-room, which looked into the court. There he would sit for hours, watching the few people who came in or went out, the post-man or some messenger bringing a letter, the grooms currying the horses—wishing that he were one of them, or even the butcher's or the grocer's boy, any one, so that he could again stand on his legs. From thence he could hear, muffled by distance, the mighty roar of the great city, the multifarious cries of the street vendors, the rattling of the carriages, the sound of horses' hoofs on the stones, and thus, as it were, mix with the flood of life moving round him. At other times he would have himself placed at one of the drawing-room windows, overlooking the so-called garden—a plot of grass surrounded by a few stunted acacias—and from thence follow the different evolutions, the loves, the quarrels, the battles of a squad of sparrows, until his eyes ached. Every leaflet of the trees, every blade of grass in the plot, he had watched shoot, he had observed grow day by day, until from the size of tiny green pellets, each so distinct from the other that he might have reckoned them, leaflets and grass blades had merged into a continuous expanse of verdant gauze spread over the acacias and the grass-plot.

It was one day in April, the sun shone gaily, the air was tepid and full of the manifold emanations of spring, the sparrows chirped gaily in the trees. It was the first time since his accident that he breathed freely, it was the first time that he felt comparatively easy. Some of the sap which pervades and animates nature at this season was fermenting in his breast; all the fibres of his being yearned—oh! how intensely!—towards freedom from his thraldom, towards health, towards life—complete life. Let the Faculty say what they would—his physicians still dissuaded him from locomotion—here was the moment, he thought, to try his chance. "I will try the water cure," said he; "I will go to Divonne." Divonne is a French village near Gex, an hour or so from Geneva, and where is to be found a world-famous hydropathic establishment. Of all the methods of cure that had been suggested to him, he had hope or faith in none save that of water. First of all, as we have already said, the bent of his disposition prepossessed him in favour of violent treatment, and those who have experienced what hydropathy is, know full well that it is no child's play. Besides, what he had heard of it and of Divonne from a quiet and not imaginative gentleman, had taken his fancy mightily. The Baron had long and patiently pored over a voluminous treatise on the "Water-cure," and the arguments in its favour, unanswerable in his eyes, not to speak of wonderful and authenticated cases of recovery recorded in the appendix of the treatise, had transformed a matter of fancy into a matter of faith. In addition to all this the journey from Paris to Divonne was not long, and, since the beginning of 1854, all by railway, an important consideration for a man in his helpless condition.

Full of his project, he lost no time in sounding his servant about it. Would he accompany him to Divonne, near Geneva, and stay with him there, probably for several months? The man made a wry face, and answered that he was not sure; he would consider about it, and give Monsieur a decided answer in a few days. The answer came in the shape of a negative as to remaining at Divonne, but the man volunteered for an extra consideration to accompany his master thither. This would not do. The Baron wanted a confidential person near him in a strange place, and one already familiar with the terrible necessities of his position. To put himself at the mercy of the first mercenary he could find at Divonne was a step to which he had an unconquerable repugnance.

Words cannot render the bitterness of his disappointment, and the intensity of his vexation. "I am a burden," thought he, "which every one shrinks from bearing. O that I had but Carlino with me!" cried the unhappy man in a fit of inexpressible anguish, his eyes raining salt tears. "O that I had him with me, everything would become easy." Strange enough! hitherto he had thought of Carlino as an abstraction out of his reach. Suddenly the idea occurred to him that Carlino was a living being, only some hundred leagues distant, and who could be easily got at. Madame Ferrolliet, he was sure, could find him. He would write to her, write to Carlino, tell him of his misery and regret, entreat him to come and help him in his dire need.

Under the spur of his strong emotion, he could brook no delay. He rung his bell (he had always one close to him), had himself wheeled to the study, and seated before a table, where all the materials for writing lay, and began to write, or rather to try to write. It was a matter of the greatest difficulty for him, and consequently one of extremely slow execution. Sensibility had so far forsaken his fingers that he did not feel the pen between them, but had to grasp it with his whole hand. The characters he penned, or rather drew, cost him a great effort, and, after all, were scarcely legible. What with the irritation consequent upon this effort, and the forced slowness of the performance, the emotion upon which he had acted cooled, and, at the end of the second line, he paused. What he had written seemed to him too explicit—almost humiliating. Carlino, in all probability, cared no more for him now than for the man in the moon; perhaps he would laugh at his effusion. Why should he so needlessly expose himself to ridicule?

Under this new impulse he desisted from writing to Carlino. A few lines to Madame Ferrolliet would be sufficient; he would simply beg her to acquaint Carlino, if she knew where he was, that his old master of the Rue Madame was ill, and well disposed to engage him as his servant again at liberal wages, paying his return journey. But no—it was false and cowardly thus to act—he would not so demean himself; he must either state the whole truth, or not write at all. Half-measures were worth nothing. And thus, too honest and upright to diplomatize, too proud to be altogether outspoken, he dismissed the matter from his thoughts.

But it would not be dismissed—it forced itself upon him, it haunted him by day and night, it demanded a settlement this way or that, but one which should satisfy his reason, and set his mind at rest. Was he to cast aside a resource which might prove his salvation, or was he to pursue it fairly and frankly, even at the risk of demeaning himself for nothing? The legitimate instinct of self-preservation pleaded victoriously against the first horn of the dilemma; the second he debated long, turning it on all sides, scanning it from all points, and coming at last to conclusions, the novelty of some of which he was the first to be surprised at. These conclusions were that, from all he knew of Carlino, he was the last person likely to expose to ridicule his former master; that, even were he to do so, little would he, the Baron, care for the laughter of a world which had forsaken him—buried him alive—and that to acknowledge one's fault, and offer some sort of reparation, could not lower but rather exalt a man. Affliction had so far been a good teacher to our Baron; the old man was fast crumbling to pieces, and on the ruins was rising a new man enlightened and purified.

Fortified by these reflections, he wrote as follows. The letter, to save writing two, which would have taken him too long, and been too great an exertion, was addressed to Madame Ferrolliet, but indirectly also to Carlino:—

"DEAR MADAME,—Be so very kind as to let Carlino know, if you know his whereabouts, that I have met with an accident which has made me a cripple, and that I have come fully to appreciate, as it deserves, the blessing of having by one's side a faithful and affectionate servant, such as he was. During the time of his service with me I was blind to this, but sorrow has opened my eyes. If Carlino can be prevailed upon to return to me, I should consider it a real blessing. I mention no terms, for obvious reasons; but I enclose a bank-note for a hundred francs to defray his *possible* journey. If he cannot agree with my request, give the amount among the poor. I cannot write more.

"Yours, very truly,
"Gaston de Kerdiat."

He had no rest till the letter was gone; then he breathed freely—all perplexity had vanished from his mind. He felt as if he had accomplished a duty, and left the issue in the hands of Providence.

CHAPTER IV.

The following day the Baron's letter reached Madame Ferrolliet, together with several others. She opened it in its turn, and, glancing at the signature, as was her habit with letters, the handwriting of which was unknown to her, wondered what the Baron could want of her. But before she had half perused the few lines, deep pity had swallowed up her wonder, and in its place a fervent wish to be of use to the poor man took possession of the good lady. It was not the news of the accident and of the Baron's sad condition that called forth her sympathies; she had long known all these facts, the local papers of Chambery having copied every paragraph relating to the occurrence and its unfortunate results, as they appeared day by day in the Paris journals. The name, rendered familiar to Savoyard ears by the Vidame's long residence in Savoy, not at that time annexed to France, and the fact of Baron Gaston being a landowner in Savoy, were two circumstances that account naturally enough for the interest in the case shown by the Savoy press. For several months there had been no further intelligence given—a silence from which Madame Ferrolliet justly argued that Monsieur de Kerdiat must be still of this world, or the papers would have recorded his death.

What touched kind-hearted Madame Ferrolliet, even to tears, was the subdued, nay, humble tone of the Baron's letter, and the acknowledgment it contained of his injustice to Carlino. What suffering must he not have gone through, thought she with true womanly logic, to be thus transformed from the haughty, imperious man she had known, to her present correspondent, the humble petitioner for Carlino's return to him! "It does him honour," she said to herself; "it proves that there is the right stuff in him;" and forthwith she began to devise how she could most quickly and safely fulfil the commission with which he had entrusted her. In point of fact, she had no other information of Carlino's whereabouts than that which she had personally communicated to the Baron in the month of October of the previous year, now seven months ago—that is, of his return to Bovino, his native place, and of his having been afterwards, during the summer, at the Baths of Acqui.

After mature consideration, it occurred to Madame Ferrolliet that no one was so likely to be acquainted with Carlino's movements as the Syndic of Bovino. Accordingly, she sent the Baron's letter in one from herself to Carlino, under cover to the Syndic, together with a few explanatory lines to the latter, mentioning the pressing nature of the enclosure, and begging that it might be forwarded or delivered to Carlino with as little delay as possible. From what we know of old of Madame Ferrolliet's kind-heartedness, we may safely guess the contents of her letter to Carlino — it was full of arguments and entreaties to the end of persuading him to comply with the Baron's request.

Immediately upon receiving Madame Ferrolliet's letter, the Mayor had gone to the house of Carlino's sister, where the young man was used to stay when at Bovino, in the expectation of finding him there. But Carlino had left for Biella, the chief town of the province, distant about two hours, just a few days before. He had been summoned thither in great haste by Signor Colletta, his late master's youngest brother. "Do you expect him back soon?" asked the Mayor. Carlino's sister replied that she was expecting his return every day, though he had said nothing to that effect — the more so as he had an unfinished piece of cloth on the loom. Upon this intelligence the Syndic, who was a man with a conscience, and who would not for the world have run the risk of the letter confided to him going astray, kept it to himself in the daily hope that Carlino would turn up. At the end of a full week, however, and no Carlino reappearing, the Mayor grew impatient, and rode to Biella to make inquiries about Carlino from Signor Colletta, who happened to be the Mayor of Biella. "Carlino is at Turin, on account of some affairs of mine," said Signor Colletta; "what do you want with him?"

"I want to give him this letter," said the Mayor of Bovino; "which I am assured is on important and pressing business."

"Leave it with me," said Signor Colletta; "I undertake that it shall reach his hands safely." The Mayor of Bovino gave it, and wrote Madame Ferrolliet an account of his having done so. Madame Ferrolliet in her turn informed the Baron of the unforeseen circumstances which had delayed her answer, adding the intelligence that Carlino was at Turin, and probably in possession of his (the Baron's) proposal, by the time the latter received hers.

But instead of forwarding the letter to Carlino at Turin, Signor Colletta put it in his desk. What could be his reasons for so doing? Was Carlino really at Turin, or where? What had been his fortunes since leaving Paris? We are going to satisfy the reader's legitimate curiosity about all these points. It will not take us long.

Carlino, on leaving Paris, went straight to Bovino, his native place, to the house of his only sister, who, together with her husband, a very skilful cloth-weaver, received him with open arms. The manufacture of cloth is the principal trade in the province of Biella, in which Bovino is situated, and Carlino had himself been a weaver in his village before entering the service of the late prefect. What with the diversion of the journey, his cordial reception by his relations, and the renewal of acquaintanceships lost sight of during four whole years, at the end of the first week Carlino's discomfiture in Paris had lost all its smart, and was only remembered by him as a bad dream. Carlino was too happily constituted to be long unhappy; not that he was forgetful of his friends, of Victorine, for instance; on the contrary, he often thought affectionately of her, and had he had the power, he certainly would have used it to better her situation. But neither the recollection of her, nor his regret at his inability to serve her, were sufficient to interfere with, or to weigh down his natural buoyancy. There are such temperaments—incomplete, plastic, if you will—would there were none worse! At the end of a few days Carlino felt, also, that doing nothing was a very dull affair; he might have gone straight to the cloth mill in Bovino, sure to be admitted there, but he preferred calling first upon Signor Colletta at Biella, *soi-disant*, to get work, but with the hope *in petto* that his former master's brother would offer him a place in his household.

Signor Colletta was a younger brother of Carlino's first master, who had died at Chambery. He was a man about forty, in person much like his deceased brother, but in all other respects widely dissimilar to that quiet, intellectual, refined relative of his. Signor Colletta, one of the first, if not the first cloth manufacturer of the province, and already very wealthy, was a sharp man of business, grinding poor people when he could do so safely; covetous of money, of influence, of distinction, in short, an ambitious man in the less favourable meaning of the word. He aimed at becoming, what his deceased brother had been, the Member for Biella, and manœuvred for that end with considerable skill. His brother's name, the name of a public man respected by all parties, was his chief mainstay and support in his political projects.

A brother could not have given a brother a heartier welcome than that vouchsafed by Signor Colletta to Carlino. He at once ordered a bottle of the oldest Nebiolo, hobnobbed with him, and literally pelted him with professions of friendship, interlarding the whole with questions about Paris, and Carlino's experiences there. They were old acquaintances of some ten years' standing, and the last time they had met had been at Chambery on the occasion of the prefect's death. At that sad epoch Signor Colletta had shown but little favour to Carlino, who had resented his coolness: but with his indomitable good-nature he had long ago passed a sponge over those disagreeable impressions. So they sat for some time in friendly converse, until Signor Colletta said at once, "By-the-bye, you come to seek for work, I'll bet a wager."

"Yes," faltered Carlino, who had expected quite another proposition.

"You shall have as much as you wish, and of the kind you prefer, here or at Bovino, as you like," continued Signor Colletta. "Old friends are old friends." Carlino said he would rather have work at Bovino. "So you shall; go and see my foreman there, say you come from me, mind," and the interview was at an end.

Signor Colletta's policy was to keep on good terms with his brother's former servant, but on no account did he intend to introduce into his household a man who had claims on his gratitude, and who one day or other might be disposed to make those claims good. So, a little abashed, Carlino went back to his village, and to the foreman of the cloth-mill there, and obtained work from that functionary, but of the kind he *did not* like best. But there was no choice to be had.

Such as it was, he accepted it, and he worked away during the whole winter.

His earnings were good, and Signor Colletta's graciousness to him unbounded whenever they met; but the sedentary life of a weaver wearied our young man in the long-run. In the spring of 1854 he was just looking about for more congenial occupation, when he learned indirectly through another weaver who had heard it from his brother, just returned to Biella from near Acqui, that servants who could speak French were wanted at the establishment of baths at Acqui. Carlino at once made application for a place there, was immediately accepted, and entered on his new functions on the 1st of May.

These functions were something indefinite. At first, Carlino was appointed to the service of the bathers who could only speak French; but in his hands what had been indefinite soon acquired a very definite meaning. In fact, it came to pass that Carlino was required to do, and actually did *every* thing for *every* bather who could not speak the *patois* of the country —an amount of work equal to that of an engine of ten-horse power. Indeed, his activity, serviceableness, and good humour had given such general satisfaction, that at the end of the season the manager of the establishment engaged him for the next one, to begin on the 1st of May, 1855. Carlino, on his side, was so pleased with this active life, with the frequent opportunities it afforded him of pouring out unchecked the flood of his zeal on the head of suffering humanity, so gratified by the good-will he met on all sides, to say nothing of the *borsa piena*, the result of voluntary contributions, which he brought home with him—so pleased, we say, was Carlino with all this, that his "ideal" underwent a slight modification in this sense, that the individual master, to whom he had hitherto wished to devote himself, merged into a collective one, such as he had found at Acqui, viz., a public which needed assistance. His ambition went no further now than to spend his summers there in the service of suffering fellow-creatures, and his winters at Bovino with his loom.

To be candid we must say that a country-woman of his, named Beata, had mainly contributed to bring about this new mood of his. Beata occupied with the lady bathers, unable to speak the patois of the country, a post identical to that of Carlino with the gentlemen in the same predicament. This Beata was a strong handsome young woman of twenty or so, and a perfect pendant to Carlino in her way, by which we mean that she also was devoured by the zeal of doing good, and gave herself no rest by day or night to achieve this object. It was this similarity of disposition that had attracted the one toward the other, and though it is difficult to conceive how they found time in their busy life to make love, certain it is that before the end of the season they were engaged, which presupposes some love-making.

Well then, towards the end of October, at the closing of the Baths of Acqui, Carlino returned to Bovino, and to his loom. So passed the winter, and spring came, and with it approached the happy moment when Carlino might exchange the loom for more active and agreeable occupation, and, above all, when he should again be under the same roof with the beloved Beata. While engrossed by such pleasant anticipations, Carlino received, from a man sent on purpose, a verbal message that Signor Colletta wanted to see him without loss of time. This occurred in the beginning of the second week of April. Carlino dressed himself in his Sunday clothes and marched off to Biella. Signor Colletta met him all smiles and cordiality, and, taking him by the hand, introduced him into his *sancta sanctorum*.

"I have to ask you to do me a service," began the gentleman.

"A hundred if within my power," replied Carlino.

"A service," resumed the other, "which requires discretion, promptitude, and tact."

"I can only answer for my desire to serve you," said Carlino.

"I know your modesty," said Signor Colletta, "but to the point. You are aware that I am an exhibitor at the Paris Universal Exhibition, which is to open on the 1st of May, that is, in three weeks. Our articles have nothing remarkable save their cheapness, which, however, is a great consideration for the less fortunate classes; and I, for one, am more proud of supplying the poor with a warm material at the lowest imaginable price than of ministering to the luxury of the rich by the manufacture of costly velvets and brocades. But this has nothing to do with my request. Perhaps you are also aware that upwards of two months ago I sent my nephew Giorgio to Paris charged to take all the steps indispensable to our firm being admitted to exhibit, and to securing a place for our goods in the Palais de l'Industrie. All this Giorgio accomplished, if I am to believe—and why should I not?—his letter dated as far back as the 11th of February, more than seven weeks ago. That was the first and last letter that I have had from my nephew. I have written several times, but have had no answer. You can easily imagine my uneasiness, first about my nephew, and then about the articles to be exhibited. Now to relieve me of this double anxiety, I want a man familiar with Paris—a man with his eyes open, and upon whose discretion I can rely; in short, such a man as you are."

"Oh! really, sir," replied Carlino, "you have too high an opinion of me."

"Not at all, not at all," protested Signor Colletta. "You must find out my nephew, and learn everything about him and our goods, and let me know the result as quickly as possible. But you must do all this, remember, without giving my nephew reason to surmise that I have sent you to look after him. Will you undertake this commission?"

"To the best of my ability I will," answered Carlino, "but I cannot dispose of my time beyond the 26th or 27th of this month, as on the 1st of May I must be at Acqui."

"Let me see," said Signor Colletta, "to-day is the 9th; in all probability you will have done all I require by the 26th or 27th. Should you find a few more days necessary, I will put you all right with the manager of the establishment at Acqui, who is my friend."

Upon this understanding, Carlino set out on the evening of the same day, duly furnished, of course, by Signor Colletta with money, and with the address of his nephew in Paris.

This Signor Giorgio, be it said *en passant*, a young man of three-and-twenty, had inherited all the fortune of his father, a Colletta unknown to this story, and that of his uncle, Carlino's first master. Signor Giorgio therefore was as rich as he was wilful, which he was in a rather superlative degree. A good part of his capital was invested in his uncle's business, and therefore it was Signor Colletta's interest to keep on friendly terms with his nephew, and to handle him with great delicacy.

Carlino did not find Signor Giorgio at his old address, but easily procured his new one at the office of the exhibitors in the Palace of Industry, where he also ascertained that all the necessary formalities had been gone through in time by Signor Giorgio; only, instead of having the place allotted for the Colletta display properly arranged and ornamented, so as to set off the articles to the best advantage, also an important part of his mission, the young man had left it as it was, thinking of nothing further but enjoying himself. This was no serious injury, as it was easily to be remedied. Carlino managed to meet Signor Giorgio as though by accident, turned the conversation on the Exhibition, and easily drew from him the avowal of his difficulties, to help him out of which he offered his services, which were gratefully accepted. Ten days were more than sufficient to make up for the time lost, and on the 24th of April Carlino could write to Signor Colletta that he considered his task as at an end, and that he intended to leave Paris on the morrow, or on the day after that. Now, Signor Colletta had already received this letter, when we saw him lock in his desk the enclosure for Carlino delivered to him by the Mayor of Bovino.

Since his arrival in Paris, Carlino had more than once thought of going to Rue Madame to see Mdlle.

Victorine, and at the same time to inquire after M. le Baron de Kerdiat, but he never could find time to put his intention into execution. But on the eve of leaving Paris, most likely for ever, the idea of going away without a visit to Mdlle. Victorine struck him as so monstrous, that he immediately took his way towards the Faubourg St. Germain.

It was nearly two in the afternoon when he knocked at the well-known *porte cochère*, which remained shut, even in the daytime, a profession of gentility, as much as to say, "Odi profanum vulgus et arceo" and went straight to the porter's lodge. Just seventeen months since he had last left that lodge to enter a *citadine* in a state of positive distraction. The portress did not recognise him, and asked who he wanted. Let us add, to be just, that her attention just then was more than divided between the new-comer and the *pot-au-feu* which she was skilfully skimming. "What! Am I so altered," exclaimed Carlino, "that you do not recognise me, Madame Perret?"

"Bonté du ciel! why, it is Monsieur Carlino," cried she in the greatest excitement. "Pray, take a seat. How glad Perret will be to see you again! I wonder where my head was not to have recollected you instantly. So here you are again in Paris."

"I am going away again to-morrow," said Carlino, "but not without saying good day to old friends. How is M. Perret, and Mademoiselle Victorine, and Monsieur le Baron?"

"Perret is well enough, thank God, bating his rheumatism. He will be here presently. Mademoiselle Victorine always the same, as thin as a ghost—little food and little sleep never fattened anybody, as far as I know. As to Monsieur le Baron, as bad as ever, if not worse. Between you and me, he is not expected to get through the year."

Carlino stood aghast. "Are you speaking of Baron Gaston, my late master?"

"Surely, don't I? Of him who looked so big and sour."

"Is it possible?" exclaimed Carlino, "What is the matter with him?"

"Why ever since his accident...."

"What accident?" interrupted Carlino.

"Why! haven't you heard of his accident? it was in all the papers. He was thrown from his horse, and thought to be dead for full twenty-four hours," and improving the occasion, Madame Perret related to Carlino *ab ovo* the melancholy story, strengthening the lugubrious tints in proportion to the effect' that she saw her narrative was producing on her listener.

Carlino sat silent for a moment after she had finished, then said, "Do you think he could or would see me? I should be glad to tell him how much...."

here his voice grew tremulous, and the tears started into his eyes.

"I never met the like of you, for returning good for evil, and I always said as much," observed Madame Perret, on whom Carlino's emotion proved infectious. "Yes, I think he would see you, unless he is in one of his fits of pain. Shall I go and let him know that you are here?"

"Yes, do, my good Madame Perret."

"Then just mind the lodge for an instant. But no. I will shut it, and you come with me. If anybody comes, they must wait," and suiting the action to the words, she shut her door, and went up to the first story, with Carlino at her heels. The door of the Baron's apartment was ajar—too often the case, judging from what she muttered about *un tas de fainéans* doing nothing but going in and out. Madame Perret motioned to her companion to wait in the ante-room, while she went in on tiptoe to the saloon. Presently she came back saying that Monsieur was in a fit of pain, but would nevertheless see Carlino. She added in a whisper, "I never saw him so low, he is wandering in his mind, fancying that he has written to you, and that he was expecting you every day. Just go in without knocking."

The Baron lay at full length on a sofa, wrapped in a dressing gown, his head supported by a heap of pillows. Nearly four months of seclusion and of suffering had written their sad tale on his shrunken form—his face pale as death, was convulsed by such intense pain, that drops of perspiration rained off his forehead. Upon Carlino's entrance he made an unsuccessful effort to raise his head, stretched forth feebly both hands, and gasped out, "Carlino!" For his life he could not have said another word, but there lay concentrated in that simple appeal, in that invocation of a name, never once pronounced before, in the tone and in the gesture, an eloquence which went straight to Carlino's heart, and stirred up all its tenderness.

"Oh, my poor master!" cried Carlino, hurrying forward and taking in his own the sufferer's hands, and both master and servant wept long and silently over those poor half dead hands.

"I knew that you would come," said at last the Baron, who was the first to recover himself. "I knew you would, I made sure of it from the time I received Madame Ferrolliet's letter. See what a blessing you bring with you. I was in a fit of pain when you came in, your presence has cut it short."

The aspect of the speaker, his words and his tone were not those of a man wandering in his mind, and yet . . . .

"May I ask," said Carlino, in some perplexity, "what Madame Ferrolliet wrote to you?"

"That my letter to her, intended as much for you, had not found you at Bovino, but that some Signor

Colletta had taken charge of it, and would forward it to you at Turin."

"I only passed through Turin on my way to Paris," replied Carlino, more puzzled than ever, "and I now know for the first time of your having written, either to Madame Ferrolliet or to me."

"Then, how do you happen to be in Paris?" asked the Baron.

Carlino told him of the business which had brought him thither, of its termination, and of his intention of returning to Italy on the morrow. The Baron's face changed fearfully on hearing this. "Oh! for God's sake," he cried, "do not forsake me now that I have found you again! It is the hand of Providence that has brought you to my assistance. I am surrounded by mercenaries who do not care a straw about me or my sufferings. Affliction has taught me all the value of an attendant like you. My whole chance of recovery lies in the water-cure of Divonne. Nobody will go there with me if you do not. Pray, pray don't forsake me in my great need!"

Deeply touched as Carlino was by this confession of helplessness, still he had too keen a sense of propriety not to be shocked by so glaring an interversion of the relative position of master and servant. He said accordingly. "Oh! Sir, you must try to dismiss from your mind all such fears of being forsaken, nobody intends to forsake you, and I, for my part, shall only be too happy to re-enter your service, and to follow you to Divonne, or anywhere else. It is not every day that a poor devil like me meets with a good master and a good place, setting aside the advantage of seeing a little of the world."

The Baron was not taken in by Carlino's kindly pretence, but said nothing, and began descanting instead at great length on his accident, his sufferings, his dear scheme of the water-cure, telling it all with that exuberance of detail, with that fond pre-occupation of self, which characterizes all persons attacked by a serious malady, and which is in itself a relief. Never was orator listened to with more sympathetic interest.

Carlino rose to go, saying, "I am afraid of tiring Monsieur; besides, I have an appointment with Signor Colletta, and some letters to write." The Baron looked disturbed, and asked, "When can you come to stay for good and all?"

"Whenever it may suit Monsieur."

"Then I would say, don't go away, but stay. However, I must not be more selfish than I can help. Let us fix for to-morrow morning at ten. By that time I shall have got rid of my present servant."

"But," said Carlino, "I should be sorry that on my account——"

"Set your heart at rest on that score," interrupted the Baron, "he is more anxious to go than I to dismiss him, which is saying a good deal. I shall smooth his exit by a douceur. *Au revoir!* do not fail to be here at ten precisely."

Carlino went to his rendezvous, where, instead of receiving Signor Giorgio's commissions for Biella, as intended, he had to make known to that young gentleman his resolve to stay where he was, and re-enter the service of his former Paris master. Out of respect for that master, he gave no further explanations. Nor was he more explicit with Signor Colletta, to whom he wrote immediately, to inform him of the step he had taken, and to beg him to interpose his good offices with the manager of the Baths at Acqui, so that his engagement with that gentleman might be amicably cancelled. He also further requested Signor Colletta to forward to his new address, Rue Madame, the enclosure he had received from the Syndic of Bovino, and, at the same time, to give him instructions with respect to the balance of money, which Signor Colletta would see, from the note of expenses now forwarded, still remained in his (Carlino's) hands. He also wrote to his sister, excusing himself for not having done so before, an omission caused by the unexpectedness and hurry of his journey, and the constant occupation which had left no time at his disposal.

His last letter was to Beata. He took it for granted in it that she would fully approve of what he had done, though it would occasion disappointment both to her and to him. "We are young and can wait," he said in concluding; "and as to the poor sufferers we used to tend in common at the baths, my absence will not prevent their having proper care from the good souls round them, whereas this poor master of mine has nobody, or at least fancies he has nobody, but me to take care of him; and then his case is so far worse than any I ever met at Acqui, that, even had he been a stranger, I feel as if I ought to have given him the preference. Only fancy a strong, active, iron-willed man of forty or so reduced to the helplessness of a babe. And the change in his mind and ways is scarcely less striking than the change in his body. The bar of steel has become like soft wax —withal so affectionate, so yielding, so meek, that it positively pains me to see it. In my opinion a master, whatever his circumstances, should always feel and act as a master."

It was past midnight before Carlino had finished his correspondence, and gone to bed. He slept very soundly, got up early as usual, and went the first thing to put his letters in the post, and then to buy himself a good supply of linen, a complete suit of clothes, and a trunk to hold these purchases. , I am a baron's valet, thought he, and I must do honour to my master. The whole of his goods and chattels when he left Biella so suddenly, consisted of the clothes on his back. This done, he returned to his inn, had a hearty breakfast, paid his bill, dressed himself in his new clothes, and drove to Rue Madame.

It was just striking nine. He tarried a little while in the *concierge's* lodge, and having ascertained that the coast was clear, namely, that his predecessor had left more than an hour ago, he went up to the first floor, entered the bedroom of his master, who was still in bed, and said with his good-humoured smile, "Here I am, to stay until Monsieur sends me away."

"If that be the case," answered the Baron, smiling in return, "I frankly warn you that you will have long to wait."

CHAPTER V.

BRIMFUL of zeal, and of the best sort, as he was, Carlino soon found out that he had not too much of it to meet the exigencies of his situation. It took him a whole week to realise the entire helplessness of his master, and all the extent and continuity of the duties devolving upon him in consequence of this helplessness. Carlino had to get his master out of bed, to wash and dress him, to wheel him about the house, to feed him, to write his letters, to keep his accounts, to read aloud to him, to be ready at every call by day and by night, to soothe him when in pain, to cheer him when desponding, to entertain him when time hung too heavily on his hands. For though the Baron's moral temperature had risen fifty per cent. in the calm atmosphere with which Carlino surrounded him, still the poor invalid would occasionally relapse into despondency, or break out into fits of impatience and *ennui*.

To all this, however, and to keeping the apartment in order to boot, Carlino, by dint of method, activity, and good humour, found means to suffice singlehanded—for the cook, an old termagant, would not give him the least assistance—but naturally at the cost of not having a spare moment for himself, by which Mdlle. Victorine was a loser. The walks to the Luxembourg garden, the sauntering along the quays, were out of the question now; even the little chats indulged in with the door ajar, when either Victorine had to pass the first story on her way up or down, or when Carlino went by the apartment of the Marquise on his way to his attic, even these were things of the past— not to be thought of in the present. Victorine must be contented with a chance "good day," or a kind inquiry after her health sent through the *concierge*. Still it was a great comfort to have him under the same roof with her, to think of his being near while she waited the return of her mistress from ball or *soirée*, to watch in the dead stillness of the night any the least noise in the apartment below, and to say to herself,

"He has had a sound sleep," or, "He has had to get up, poor soul!"

In course of time there came by post a packet addressed to Carlino. It contained Signor Colletta's answer to Carlino's last letter, and the often-mentioned letter from Madame Ferrolliet. Signor Colletta, having first explained the delay of the enclosure, thanked and complimented Carlino on the speedy and happy issue of the business entrusted to his care, approved of his expenses, and begged him to accept, as a mark of the writer's satisfaction, a hundred francs, to be deducted from the balance still remaining in Carlino's hands, the surplus, at a convenient moment, to be returned to Signor Giorgio. The contents of Madame Ferrolliet's packet we already know—a letter from the Baron to Madame Ferrolliet, and one from her to Carlino, with the bank-note for a hundred francs intended for Carlino's journey.

This note was nearly the cause of a disagreement between master and servant. Carlino returned it to the Baron, insisting that he had no right to it; the Baron, on his side, refusing to receive it. "It was meant for your journey. Have you not read my letter to Madame Ferrolliet? It belongs to you!"

Carlino received this assertion on the horns of a dilemma. "If it was for my journey, it is not needed, as here I am in Paris with my expenses defrayed by Signor Colletta; if you mean it as a present to me,

I cannot accept it, for I have had no time to deserve it."

"I decline being under an obligation to Signor Colletta," said the Baron.

"You are under none," said Carlino.

"Well then, nor to you," retorted the Baron, chafing. "That is," he continued, checking himself, "no more than I can help." The Baron had controlled his temper at sight of a cloud overcasting Carlino's face. He added in a gentle tone, "You know that I am under more obligations to you than money can pay. Come, come, take it, if only not to pain me."

Carlino took it out of obedience, though he would have given much not to be obliged to do so. Though Carlino was not greedy of money, he understood the value of it, now especially that he had matrimony in view. His repugnance in this case had its rise in the feeling that he had really done nothing to earn this hundred francs, and in the misgiving that the Baron might fancy he did out of interested motives what he had the consciousness of doing from the promptings of his own heart.

The Baron's all-absorbing preoccupation at this moment was his journey to Divonne. He could think and talk of nothing else. He was never tired of demonstrating, scientifically, as he thought, book in hand, the excellence of the water-cure system, the strengthening action of water upon the tissues, the consequent rebound of the tissues upon the nerves, &c. Carlino wished for nothing better than to believe—and, indeed, the expounder's faith in his panacea was so entire that it communicated itself to the simple mind of the listener, with a reservation, however, in favour of the mud-baths of Acqui. The servant also had his miraculous cures to relate, to which the master would listen in his turn, with that eager interest and credulity with which all but hopeless invalids suck in, as it were, everything that can nourish their delusion of some way to recovery.

There was that in the mud-baths of Acqui, as described by Carlino, which took the Baron's fancy, and chimed in with his natural predilection for extreme remedies. To have one's body covered with a stratum of intensely hot mud, to be left to stew under that kind of coat until the perspiration trickled in rivulets from every pore, struck our sufferer as a sufficiently heroic process to be likely to produce some results, and therefore worth trying. "But your Acqui," would the Baron observe, "has one defect—it is so far off, and no railway to it. We must put off our going there until a better opportunity—if that ever comes. Should Divonne do me good, I mean so far as to restore the partial use of my limbs—I say only partial—you see I am not over sanguine or exacting—well, if Divonne only succeeds in restoring me to be half a man, nothing need then hinder us from going to Acqui."

"Just so," assented Carlino; "Divonne is to be our first stage to Acqui."

"And the sooner we get to Divonne," added the Baron, "the sooner we shall get to Acqui."

Master and servant being thus of one mind, all that remained for Carlino was to push forward the preparations for their intended journey and long stay at the famous hydropathic establishment.

Things were at this crisis when one morning that *rara avis*, a visitor, arrived. It was the doctor who had chanced to be on the spot when the Baron's accident had occurred, and who had brought him home, to all appearance dead. He had been in attendance for a month professionally, and afterwards had continued to drop in at long intervals, unprofessionally. A spare, tall gentleman, of middle age, who talked little, but to the point, and had a quiet, sympathetic manner, which inspired confidence. Baron Gaston was grateful to the doctor for the interest he had continued to show, and always saw him with pleasure. As for Carlino, he lost his heart to the physician at first sight. His service obliging him to go in and out of the room where the gentlemen were, he could not but catch some driblets of their conversation. The Baron announced to the doctor his approaching departure for Divonne. "Ah, indeed!" was the rejoinder, in a tone that seemed to Carlino anything but approving. Then, again, he heard the doctor say, as he was taking leave, "I wish you a good journey and success; but, above all, be on your guard against the wet—it is a pity that you cannot wait till the warm weather sets in."

Carlino accompanied the doctor to the door, and said to him, "Excuse the liberty, sir, but do you really think the water-cure will benefit my master?"

"Why, my friend," said the doctor, "you ask me more than I can tell; harm it probably will not do."

"And," asked Carlino again, "perhaps it were better not to go so soon?"

"As to that, you are quite right," answered the doctor. "You seem to be attached to your master, therefore I will venture to tell you frankly, that every day's delay will be a clear gain to the Baron; but if he insists, and gets angry, go. To keep his mind easy is the thing of all things for him."

Too conscientious to disregard the doctor's warning, and too far committed to the speedy realisation of the water-cure scheme, to stop midway without any good reason to give, Carlino was never more perplexed in his life. Happily chance, as sometimes happens in similar straits, came to his aid. May proved very stormy and wet, and when the fine weather did set in, it came accompanied by a biting north wind. These meteorologic circumstances were pleaded by Carlino with tolerable success, and the Baron submitted to the delay without overmuch fretting or fuming. But there is an end to everything, especially to wet and cold in May; and there came a day, towards the end of the month, when the sun shone bright and warm, and the barometer stood fixed at fine weather. It was on the 26th that the Baron said to Carlino, "It is to-day a month since you re-entered my service; here are your wages for that time."

Carlino took the money, and saw at a glance that it amounted to a hundred francs. "Monsieur pays me as much as when I kept myself, which is not just," observed Carlino.

"Never mind," replied the Baron, "you have now at least double work, and I choose to pay you in proportion to your work."

"Dear me, I shall grow a miser," protested Carlino, pitifully; "the other day it was a hundred francs from Signor Colletta, then another hundred from Monsieur, and now a hundred again. What shall I do with all this money?"

"It will be of use to you when you are no longer in my service."

"Does Monsieur mean to send me away?"

"You know well that I do not intend that, Carlino; I mean that I shall leave you—die one of these days, and then——"

"I beg Monsieur not to speak so, even in jest."

"I speak in sober earnest," was the Baron's reply. "What can I expect to do but to die, if nobody, not even you, will help me to make a trial of what may save me?" The reproach, not entirely undeserved, cut Carlino to the quick.

"Monsieur knows that I am ready to obey him."

"Yes, you said as much a month ago, and here we are still."

"Shall I go and bespeak a bed-carriage for to-morrow?"

"Not for to-morrow, but for the day after, if you have no objection."

"Bless my heart! what objection can I have? It is for Monsieur to order, and for me to obey," and away went Carlino to finish the packing. In the course of the day a thought occurred to him, which he communicated to his master,—the thought that it might be as well to write to Divonne, so as to ensure rooms. The Baron agreed to this, to make assurance doubly sure, as he said; but would not hear of writing, and telegraphed instead. On the same evening a telegram in answer arrived, to say that the rooms applied for were at his disposal. On the morrow a *coupé-lit* was secured, and on the following day they started.

For you and me to start, who have the full use of our limbs, is a simple matter enough; to drive to the station, have the luggage registered, get a ticket, and then seek for the most comfortable seat in a railway carriage—all this does not require much exertion, nor does it take much time. But for a poor creature who can do nothing for himself to start, is a long and complicated operation, fraught with much difficulty and much misery of mind and body. It was an affair of state for our helpless traveller to be carried down-stairs to the court, and there lifted into a coach; and a second affair of state to be lifted out of the coach, carried like a bundle to the platform, and from thence transferred to the bed-carriage. The material discomfort of being thus hauled about, considerable as it was, shrunk to nothing in comparison to the mental torture of feeling himself the object of the idle curiosity, not unmixed with pity, if you will, but not the less offensive for that, which stared at him from all the windows of the house he was leaving, which gathered round him in groups, both at the Paris terminus and at that of Geneva. Few know, save those who have gone through such an ordeal, to what extent bodily infirmity is shy, and how it is apt to writhe under exposure; few know the exquisite pain which a look or a gesture can inflict. Carlino did all he could to screen his master from the gaze of indiscreet onlookers, and to divert his thoughts from it, with more zeal than success. At last the herculean task was accomplished. Divonne was reached; and worn and weary, but thankful at heart, the Baron was safely lodged in the comfortable suite of apartments bespoken by telegraph.

Three cheerful rooms full of light and air, opening on a wavy expanse of variegated green, gentle slopes of pasture, rich stretches of purple forest, in short, on all that is best calculated to gladden the eyes and heart of a poor recluse. The transition from the dingy apartments in Rue Madame, with its lookout on a few meagre trees to this vast luxurious prospect, floating in an atmosphere of diamond-like purity, had something magical in it, it resembled a dream, and of the best sort. The Baron was enraptured, his sensations were those of a person long buried in a subterranean dungeon, who is suddenly restored to freedom, and the light of day. His spirits rose high. If the mere aspect of the country, thought he, if the fresh air he breathed, sufficed to revive him, what had he not the right to expect from those wholesome agencies when combined with a treatment, the efficaciousness of which was an article of faith with him?

His impatience to begin may be easily conceived, but in this he was checked. The faculty which ruled at the baths decided that he must first have a week of complete repose. At the end of the week, the treatment commenced, but in its mildest form—wet bandages and sheets in which he was made to lie down for an hour between blankets, twice a day, submitting afterwards to a gentle rubbing. This was a mere trifle, next to nothing of what was to follow; but even this little was productive of beneficial results. Not that the great enemy, palsy, to call it by its right name, had in the least given way, but the patient's general health had improved. The little he ate, he ate without repugnance, now and then even with pleasure, his sleep was better and more refreshing, no longer haunted by horrible dreams. And then, he had no fits of pain since his arrival. All this was so much ground gained, and moreover, full of good augury for a more decisive success.

The hours which were not taken by the watercure, and by his meals (these were served to him in his apartments), the Baron spent at the window. Sometimes he had himself carried down to the garden, made the tour of it in his wheeled-chair, or had himself so placed, that his head was in the shade, the rest of his body in the sun. There were plenty of attendants within call to carry him up and down stairs; but once in the garden Carlino attended him exclusively, wheeling him here and there, reading or talking to him, according to the fancy of the moment.

The Baron was not the only inmate of the establishment deprived of the power of motion, and consequently dependent on others for all locomotion. With those in the same sad plight as himself he willingly exchanged greetings, and compared notes *en passant*, but never conversed long with any one. He instinctively shrunk from confidences which might shake his faith or dim his hopes. Some of the patients hopped about on crutches, or walked leaning on the arms of attendants. How he envied them! So true is it that everything is relative. One unhappy being, a young lady of nineteen or twenty, was worse than he was. She could not sit upright in her garden chair, but had to be wheeled about in a recumbent position. This poor young victim of a chronic disease was the only fellow-sufferer in whom the Baron took an interest.

It was not till the first week of July that he was considered seasoned enough to bear the brunt of a more heroic phase of the system. To the wet bandages and sheets was now added an alternatively cold and lukewarm douche at six in the morning, the power of which was gradually raised, then a good deal of friction, followed by a rest in bed. Late in the afternoon, ablutions and rubbing again. Three weeks of this regimen considerably reinvigorated him, his appetite grew keener, his sleep longer and quieter, and . . . was it a delusion, or was it a reality? It seemed to him as if his hands were no longer so benumbed as heretofore. He observed himself closely and incessantly, watched and compared the state of his hands day by day, nay, hour by hour, with what anxiety God only knows—at last he could no longer be blind to the fact that they were improving.

"Look here," said he one day to Carlino, "a fortnight ago I could not close my fist, and now you see I can nearly do so."

"The Lord be thanked!" cried Carlino; "have I not told Monsieur a thousand times that he would get better?" and forgetting for a moment, in the excitement of his joy, all respect for his master, Carlino cut a caper, which did as much honour to the elasticity of his legs as to the goodness of his heart.

"If I do get better," said the Baron with something glistening in his eyes, "it will be to you, after God, that I shall owe it."

Carlino said nothing in answer, for, addicted as he was to the melting mood, to articulate a word just then, and to give way, would have been one and the same thing, but the sudden glow over his features, and his glance of affection towards his master, said clearly enough how such an assurance had rejoiced his soul.

Carlino seized this occasion to fulfil a promise he had made to Mademoiselle Victorine, viz., to write to her. He had not done so before, for the excellent reason that he had had nothing agreeable to impart. But having now pleasant news, which he knew would rejoice his correspondent, he sat down to his master's desk, now given over to him in his character of secretary, and spent one of the hours of the Baron's siesta, following the morning douche, in telling Mademoiselle Victorine about the journey, his own impressions of the establishment, and specially giving an account of his master's health. The two hours of the Baron's siesta were Carlino's only leisure time, that is to say, the only part of the day in which he was not actually employed about the Baron's person. For as to going out alone, or losing sight of the invalid only for ten minutes, there was no question of it. Even during the douche and other manipulations, Carlino was always present. The care of the apartment and the waiting on his master at meal-times also devolved upon him exclusively.

Well, the letter had been gone ten days, and yet no answer. This rather disturbed Carlino, who knew what a capital pen-woman Mademoiselle Victorine was, and how much time she unluckily had at her disposal during the small hours of the night. The answer came at last, and told a sad tale. Mademoiselle Victorine was no longer with the Marquise, no longer in the Rue Madame, but in the passage Tivoli, where Carlino's letter had at last reached her. Her mistress had discharged her five weeks ago, refusing to give her a good character, and thus frustrating all her efforts to procure a new situation. She was now living with her mother in the passage Tivoli, a very poor and low neighbourhood, and in great distress about her old and infirm parent, for whom she had no longer the means of procuring little comforts.

This letter kept Carlino from sleeping; he spent

the whole night in trying to devise some means of helping his friend, until by dint of thinking, he at last hit upon a scheme, which would extricate her from her sad situation. Accordingly, the first thing he said to his master the next morning, was, "I have had a letter from Mademoiselle Victorine, and I am sorry to say it brings very sad news."

"Who is Mademoiselle Victorine?" asked the Baron.

"The *femme de chambre* of the Marquise," explained Carlino.

"Some young and handsome girl, that you patronise, you rogue!" laughed the Baron, who was in the best of humours.

"Neither young nor handsome," retorted Carlino, "simply a worthy creature most shamefully treated;" and in a few but feeling words he told his master Mademoiselle Victorine's pitiful story, and then read him her letter.

"I don't see anything we can do for her," said the Baron, "but send her some money."

"I think Monsieur might help her in a permanent way. When we go back to Paris, Monsieur will want a cook" (the Baron before quitting home had dismissed the termagant who reigned in his kitchen, and left the apartment to the care of the *concierge*): "why should not Monsieur engage Mademoiselle Victorine as cook?"

"Why, my good fellow, because your friend is a *femme de chambre*, and I shall require a cook."

"But I know that she can cook tolerably well, and what she does not know she can learn while we are here. Then I can cook, and can assure Monsieur that between us, Monsieur shall not starve for want of good meals. Besides, Mademoiselle Victorine is a capital needlewoman, and can look after Monsieur's linen;" and as a clencher, Carlino wound up his peroration with, "she is so good and so miserable!"

The Baron allowed himself to be persuaded, and by the post of the same day, Carlino had the satisfaction of informing Victorine of the scheme he had contrived for her, and of its full success with his master. "After all," he wrote in conclusion, "the condition of a cook is as honourable as that of a lady's maid, or rather, as my former master used to say, all conditions are alike honourable when honourably discharged. So I hope you will have no objection to our cooking in partnership for our master." Then he added in a P.S., "Here enclosed are two bank-notes for a hundred francs each: consider them as an advance on your wages, which will help you to keep your mother comfortable for the present, and also to pay for some lessons in cooking." The wording of this P.S., so as to leave it doubtful who sent the money, had cost Carlino much time and contention of mind, but nevertheless his finesse was yet to turn against himself.

The answer to this epistle was not long in coming this time, and we may trust the reader for guessing the tenor of its contents. Only it did not come alone, but with a letter of thanks addressed directly to the Baron, in which much gratitude was expressed for the two hundred francs he had so kindly advanced. Victorine had taken it for granted, from the largeness of the sum, that it must come from the Baron.

"And so," said the Baron, "you sent your *protégée* two hundred francs?"

Carlino, taken unawares, reddened as though he had been caught with his hand in his master's pocket, and answered, "Yes, sir."

"It was scarcely a fair proceeding," resumed the Baron, "especially as the first notion of sending her money came from me. And then why does she plague me with her thanks?"

"I suppose I did not make it clear who sent the money," said Carlino; "nay, to tell the truth, I know I did not."

"And why, pray?" asked the Baron.

"I was afraid Mademoiselle Victorine would refuse the money if she knew it came from me, and . . . ."

"And so I broadly intimated that it came from my master," said the Baron, finishing the sentence for Carlino.

"No, I hinted nothing of the kind," protested Carlino. "I only told Mademoiselle Victorine to consider the money as an advance of her wages."

"Which was tantamount to saying," retorted the Baron, "that it came from the giver of the wages, that is, from me. I see you are not the fellow-countryman of Macchiavelli for nothing, but your macchiavellism shall not avail you much this time. Since I am to have the benefit of this good action, I mean Mademoiselle Victorine's thanks, it is only just and right that I should deserve them."

And so Carlino's scheme was defeated, and he had to take back his two hundred francs. After all it is not probable that his macchiavellism lowered him much in his master's estimation.

It was now the middle of August, and the heat tremendous, but far from being incommoded by it, Baron Gaston rather enjoyed it. One night, let us premise that he had never gone to bed in a more hopeful frame of mind, forming all sorts of plans for the future, devising alterations in the castle, in one word talking like one who has an indefinite lease of life; well, one night Carlino was scared out of his sleep by a great cry from his master. Carlino slept on a camp-bed in the dining-room, close to the door of the Baron's bedroom, with the door open between the two rooms. In a twinkling he had lighted a candle, and was by his master's bedside. "What is the matter, Monsieur?"

"The thunder, haven't you heard the thunder? It burst right over my bed—see if the coverlid is not on fire." He looked aghast as he spoke, and his hair stood on end with terror.

"There is not the least trace of fire," said Carlino after examining the bed-clothes; "I have heard no noise whatever;" and then opening a window he added, "The stars are shining bright, not a cloud in the sky. You must have been dreaming, sir."

"It was no dream, I can tell you; I saw as plainly as I see you a ball of fire rush along and fall on my bed, I heard the crash, I felt the shock."

Carlino did not choose to dispute the point further, and applied himself instead to soothe his master's agitation, in which he so far succeeded that the Baron again dropped asleep, when Carlino crept cautiously back to his own bed.

Apprised in the morning of the incident of the night, the doctor paid the Baron an early visit, questioning him minutely, and wearing a graver face than was warranted by the relation of a dream. The Baron complained of a very strange feeling, a feeling of anxiety, as though something was about to happen to him, with besides painful twitches and twinges all through his body, even in those parts which had long lost all sensibility. The doctor advised him not to get up, and forbade the douches, at least for the present. A more unwelcome order could not have fallen on the Baron's ear; to interrupt the water-cure was to take from him his last anchor of hope. "'The air is full of electricity," said the doctor, "a storm is impending, and I do not at all wonder in the oversensitive state of your nerves they should have given you warning, some hours beforehand, of what is coming." In fact, huge white clouds were rising up from behind the mountains, and that ominous stillness pervaded the air which is the forerunner of some great convulsion of nature.

From the kind of symptoms complained of by his master, Carlino dreaded that he was about to have one of his fits of excruciating pain. Nor had he long to remain in suspense. A short time after the doctor's visit the attack came on, bearable for the first two hours, ending in a torture of unprecedented violence. The pain, vague and general at first, or only momentarily circumscribed and shifting its place, ended as usual by localizing itself in a very small compass, not above the size of half-a-crown, and then the agony of agonies ensued. It was fearful to hear the poor sufferer's cries, fearful to see him writhe and twist and bound from his couch, like an adder trod upon. No sedatives were of any avail, the utmost devotion could bring no relief. Such was the intensity of the spasm that he could not bear to be spoken to, nor even endure that Carlino should approach his bed, but by insensible degrees and with the gentlest circumspection. Carlino, who had never seen him half so bad, and who felt he could do him no good, had no other resource but that of tears. The violence of the attack only began to abate towards five o'clock in the afternoon—it had lasted seven hours. By six it was entirely over, its disappearance coinciding with the bursting forth at last of the long-threatening storm. An appalling one it was, the sky a continuous sheet of fire, thunder-clap succeeding thunder-clap without intermission, and accompanied by floods of rain. Carlino sat up all night by his master's bedside, who was so exhausted as scarcely to be able to ask for a sip of water. Towards morning he had some hours of broken sleep.

From that terrible day might be dated a rapid and continual regression for our patient; not only did he lose in less than a week all that he had gained in ten, —renewed strength, better appetite, sounder sleep, &c., —but in many points he was now far worse than when he came. His strength, for instance, had considerably declined, and the condition of his hands and arms was decidedly impaired from what it was at Paris, and was impairing every day. The doctor persisted in his veto, nay, gave it clearly to be understood that he should not authorise the resumption of the water-cure short of certain contingencies, which were not likely to arise.

Carlino one morning found his master in tears, bitter, desolate tears. "I weep over my last poor illusion," said the Baron, as soon as the paroxysm allowed him to speak. "You remember my showing you my hands not six weeks ago, and my triumph at being almost able to close my fist? Look at them now—they are straight open, and no effort of my will can so much as bend the first joint of even my little finger, motion and sense of touch alike gone, wooden hands and arms. All is dead in me but my head; it would be a real mercy to strike it off, and be done with it. If you loved me wisely you would put an end to me, Carlino." And, seeing poor Carlino's consternation, he added, "Oh! if you could understand all my misery! But you cannot; oh! why was I born? why was I born?"

For the two or three next days he scarcely spoke, or even raised his eyes. They were riveted on the ground, he seemed lost in a brown study. All Carlino's ingenious devices to draw him out of his gloomy reflections, to find some interest or diversion, were unavailing. "Thank you for your good intentions," he would say, "but I have sunk so low that even your affection, your great and noble affection, finds no responsive chord in my heart. Leave me quiet. I am solving a great problem."

He said one evening, rousing himself from a long reverie, "Carlino, take me back to Paris, render me this last service."

"Why does Monsieur say *last?*" asked Carlino, with some uneasiness.

"Never do you mind why," replied the Baron. "Invalids past hope are apt to have presentiments, or fancies, if you like that better. Take me back to Paris."

"It is for Monsieur to order, and for me to obey," said Carlino; "but Monsieur will allow me to say that he will find the apartment in the Rue Madame very close and dingy in comparison with these gay rooms, this beautiful view, and this fine air."

The Baron was sitting by the open window, Carlino by his side. It was a calm September evening, all round passing lovely to look upon. There was that mellowness of tints, the despair of painters, peculiar to the season. Autumn had begun its luxuriant patchwork of gold and purple on mountain and vale. The redbreast chased from the heights by the chilly nights had grown domestic, and uttered its silvery chirp near the house. The Baron contemplated the landscape with a look of scorn, and exclaimed, "I loathe this feast of nature; to me, for whom hope does not colour it, all this beauty is a mockery and an insult. Let us go to Paris. My dingy rooms in the Rue Madame will be a fitter preparation for another abode far more dingy and cold and narrow."

Carlino made a last effort. Convinced that if his master were allowed to resume his water-cure he would remain at Divonne, and his hopes again revive, Carlino went to the doctor, and besought him, if the thing were possible, besought him with tears, to recall his veto, or at least fix a period, not too far off, for its withdrawal. But his prayers were of no avail. The doctor pleaded his responsibility, and was unmovable.

So there was nothing for it but to pack and go. They went. Of what use to describe that journey? It was as trying and cumbrous, and fraught with as many difficulties as had been that from Paris to Geneva. Only this time the Baron seemed to be little or not at all discomposed by that exposure to the public gaze, which he had felt so keenly on the previous occasion. It might be that he was too much absorbed to take much notice of the gaping crowd, or that he looked down upon them from the height of one of those resolutions in the face of which everything below seems small and insignificant.

They were received in the Rue Madame by Victorine, who, telegraphed to in time by Carlino, had taken possession of the apartment during the last forty-eight hours, had put it in order, lighted the fires, and prepared everything necessary for the travellers.

Her new master hardly noticed her, and she with much discretion kept in the background. Indeed, the Baron's fatigue and exhaustion were so great, that he went immediately to bed, had a potage and two new laid eggs, and then said he would try to sleep. Carlino went to his bedside twenty times at least during the night, and always found him sleeping soundly.

CHAPTER VI.

"I DO not ask if Monsieur slept well, for I know he did," said Carlino next morning in high glee.

"Perfectly," replied the Baron. "It is said that the Prince of Condé never slept so soundly as on the eve of the battle of Rocroi."

"But you had no battle in view," said Carlino.

"Who knows!" sighed the Baron, and a shade of unspeakable sadness passed over his face. He remained with his eyes closed for a minute in deep meditation; then rousing himself he said—"Take that bunch of keys lying on the table, the largest but one opens the drawers of the bureau in the study, unlock the second drawer and bring it to me."

Carlino did as he was bid. The drawer in question was brimful of papers methodically arranged and tied up in bundles of various sizes. Two small pocket-pistols peeped from beneath some papers. Actuated by no distinct motive, for in his master's helpless condition all the weapons in Christendom might have lain by his side without the least danger of his using them, Carlino took the pistols out, and then carried the drawer to his master.

"Lay it on my bed here—there were two small pistols on the top, what have you done with them?"

"They seemed to me to want cleaning," said Carlino, "and so I took them away."

"Were you afraid that I should blow out my brains with them?" asked the Baron with a sinister look and laugh, both painful to hear and to see.

"Monsieur has a way of jesting which saddens me to death," said Carlino, with a touch of reproach in his voice.

"Well, well—don't find fault. I will sadden you no more. Now put your hand under that big bundle there, tied with pink ribbon, and you will find a small packet in blue paper—that's it, undo it."

Carlino unfolded the several blue covers of the packet, and came at last to a small phial full of brownish liquid. "Open it," said the Baron. Carlino removed the glass stopper with some difficulty, and immediately recognised the smell of opium, with which his experience at Acqui had made him familiar.

"It is laudanum!" he exclaimed.

"Indeed!" said the Baron; "let me see if you are right, bring it nearer. I don't smell it yet—raise my head higher—now let me smell it," and the moment the open phial was on a level with his mouth, he made a snatch at it with his teeth.

"Oh! Saints of Paradise," exclaimed the horrified Carlino, drawing the bottle back in time, "he wants to kill himself!"

"And so I will and shall!" cried the Baron, in a burst of fury. "Give me the bottle, I tell you; I command you to give it to me this instant. If you don't, I will starve myself." Then, after a pause, he resumed in a more pacific tone, "Listen to me, Carlino. You see that bundle of papers under which lay the phial. Those papers are Piedmontese bonds, worth thirty thousand francs; take them, put them in your pocket, they are yours, but let me have the bottle."

"Oh, sir," cried Carlino, in a tone impossible to convey; "oh, sir, I have not deserved this from you!" and trembling from head to foot he fell on a chair half fainting, and hiding his face in his hands, began to cry desperately.

The Baron watched Carlino with a look of inexpressible fondness till his eyes also filled, and tears rolled fast and thick down his wan cheeks. It would have been difficult to decide which of the two actors in this heart-rending scene was the most to be pitied. At last the Baron said, said it most softly, "Forgive me, Carlino, I didn't know what I said. It was wrong of me to try and bribe you into doing what I ought only to expect from your affection for me, from your good sense, from your pity. It is to these I now appeal. Reflect on my state, my good Carlino, my best friend. Was there ever a more unhappy, a more hopeless one? I am a living corpse shut up already in a coffin—a burden to myself and others, debarred not only from all the pleasures of life, from all that makes it worth having, but from what is indispensable to make existence tolerable. Most of its ordinary functions are taken from me. I am as incapable of moving as a log, I cannot read without turning giddy, I cannot eat, I cannot sleep. My eyes and ears are, it is true, unimpaired, but of what use are either? My visible world, owing to my helplessness, is confined to the court-yard and garden of this house, and as for my hearing, it only serves me so far as to follow the squabbles of the grooms below. Is such a life, if it can be called life, worth keeping? But even these are not all my miseries—amid so many disabilities, there survives within me, fresh and whole, a fatal capability for suffering, for unlimited suffering. God is my witness that I have borne it as long as it was bearable, but it is so no longer. The mere thought of another such fit of pain as my last at Divonne maddens me. Now I put it to you, Carlino, had you a dog in the state I have just described, would you not in common humanity put him out of his suffering?"

"But a dog has no soul to be saved, and you have—think of that, my dear master," objected Carlino.

"God Almighty will have mercy on my soul," retorted the Baron. "God Almighty, who bestowed on the camel the instinct by which it throws off its burden when too heavy, cannot punish me for not bearing what is unbearable, for not doing what is impossible. Self-preservation is the natural law of our being, but where that law ceases to operate, there is an end to all responsibility, there begins the right to do away with oneself. Don't you see this? It is self-evident."

"Listen to me, my dear master," said Carlino, falling on his knees by the bedside, and speaking with solemn earnestness. "You are a gentleman of education and learning, and speak like one. I am only a poor ignorant peasant, therefore unfit to argue with you. I can only go by what I have been taught, and beginning with the good priest who taught me my catechism, down to my late master, who was a very clever and pious man, I have always been warned that for a man to kill himself is a mortal sin, that the Church refuses her prayers and Christian burial to such as have done so, and that they go straight to hell, where a great countryman of mine, privileged by God to journey through hell, purgatory, and paradise while yet alive, saw them with his own eyes, and left record of what he saw in a famous book, that my late master was never tired of reading over and over again.

Believing all this as I do, how can Monsieur expect that I should help him to his eternal perdition? But even if I did not believe what I have been taught, even if supposing Monsieur could persuade me, how could I, loving Monsieur as I do, ever take a part in killing him?"

"And so, out of mistaken affection, you condemn me to die by a slow fire, inch by inch? I had hoped better things from your attachment. It would be better if you hated me, since your attachment stands in the way of my deliverance."

"In the name of all that is holy, my dear master, make an effort, and try to get rid of these unnatural ideas. They come from the devil. Prayer will conjure them away. Let us pray, Monsieur," and Carlino crossed himself and began to recite the Paternoster.

"Spare me your mummery and your presence," interrupted the Baron, "I would rather be alone."

"Will Monsieur not get up?"

"No, no; go."

Carlino went to cry his eyes out in the kitchen, by the side of the scarcely less distressed Mademoiselle Victorine.

We owe the reader a word of elucidation. Baron Gaston, we have stated it before, had formed the resolution not to survive the loss of all hope of recovery. . Looking forward to this dread possibility, he had long previously loaded to the muzzle the pair of pocket pistols which we have discovered in one of the drawers of his escritoir. It was only at a later period that the fear had crossed his mind that his hands might get so far worse as to disable him from pulling the trigger of a pistol. Then he had thought of secreting the small phial of laudanum in question, as offering more facility for the accomplishment of his design than any weapon. Small doses of opium, either as a sedative for his pains or as a soporific, had been frequently administered to him since his accident.

It is painful to have to say that the Baron's resentment against Carlino proved both bitter and lasting. It oozed out of his sullen silence, of his angry looks, of his sharp monosyllables. All his former liking for his faithful servant had been replaced by dislike. It seemed at times as if the mere sight of that good-natured face was too much for him. "What necessity is there for your mounting guard over me all day?" would he suddenly say. "Have you nothing to do elsewhere? Are you afraid that I should profit by your absence, to throw myself out of window?" And the moment Carlino had turned his back, he called after him, reproaching him with never being at hand. The poor man took a mischievous pleasure in crossing and finding fault with his servant. Whatever Carlino proposed, no matter what, were it only the opening or shutting of a window, the Baron was sure to say "No." If Carlino hazarded a gentle remonstrance, he was denounced as a tyrant; if he protested his attachment, and called God to witness that he would willingly bear half his master's cross, he was convicted of hypocrisy. Forsooth, it was easy to make fine speeches, when they pledged you to nothing! Even Carlino's buoyancy and sanguineness of disposition—and they were not what they had been—were not proof against this incessant persecution. He lived literally on tears; his sleep and appetite were gone. This terrible phase of his master's temper left such an indelible impression on the poor fellow's mind that, even in after years, he could not allude to it, or even think of it, without shuddering. The trial, thank God, was not long.

Monsieur de Kerdiat awoke one morning as if from a nightmare—awoke quite another man from the one of the day before. The first words he said to Carlino were, "Are you not yet tired of lavishing so much care on a brute like me?"

"Oh, how can Monsieur say such things?"

"I am wrong; brutes behave themselves better. I have seen even wild beasts show some gratitude to the one who fed them. Can you forgive me, Carlino?"

Carlino could say neither yes nor no, for the tears that suffocated him.

"My only excuse," continued the Baron, "is that I did not know what I was doing. Really at times I am not responsible for what I say or do. I have followed your advice, my good Carlino—I have prayed. I have tried hard many a time without result, but I have succeeded at last. Prayer has cleared my disordered intellect, has softened my proud, hard heart. I never knew before what a blessing, what a power resides in prayer. I understand now what impious, what criminal things I have asked of you. I see and feel how right you were in refusing to listen to me. You have been my guardian angel, Carlino. It is useless to try and stop me; I will speak out what I have at heart to say. If I die like a man and a Christian, as I am resolved to do, I shall owe it to you. Henceforward you shall guide me; I resign my will into your hands. You know, far better than I do, what is good for me and what is not. From this moment you are no longer to ask me if I will do this or that, but simply to say, 'Do this or that'—do you promise?"

"Why, if I do, Monsieur," replied Carlino, smiling through his tears, "we shall, I am sure, make a great mess of it; for if ever there was a man born to obey and not to command, that man is Monsieur's humble servant."

"Well," counterargued the Baron, with a smile in return, "if you are born to obey, then I command you to tell me always what I am to do, and you cannot go against my command."

"I must do my best," said Carlino. "Suppose Monsieur was to take his breakfast, and then get up?"

Both these operations being concluded, so long and laborious that of the dressing, that it had to be followed by an hour of complete repose, Carlino further proposed a visit to the cook, "a member of Monsieur's establishment, whom Monsieur had never taken any notice of," and on the Baron agreeing both to the accusation and to the proposal, he was wheeled into the kitchen, where he had a good long chat with Victorine, apologising to her for not having seen her before, and thanking her for all the good things she had concocted for him. "I wish to see more of you," said the Baron, as he was wheeled away, "nay, I shall like to have a chat with you whenever you have any spare time."

To see him look so kindly, to hear him speak so gently, after those three interminable weeks of angry, gloomy silence, it was scarcely possible to believe that it was the same man. Carlino was half-crazy with joy, and hardly knew what he was about; so much so, indeed, that a few hours later, while arranging his own room, when he took out of its case, and, according to custom, rubbed his harmonica till it shone like gold, he so far forgot himself as to put it to his lips, and sent forth a wave of sound. It was the first time he had done this since resuming his service with the Baron. The sound half scared him. He felt the blood mount to his face, hastily shut up the instrument, and returned to his master in the study.

"Did you hear the music?" asked the Baron.

"I did, sir," faltered Carlino; "I hope it did not disturb you?"

"On the contrary, it pleased me; it was only a simple chord, but sweet and melancholy. It made me think of the æolian harps in the old castle at Baden. What could it be?"

"If Monsieur is curious to know," replied Carlino smiling, "I can introduce him both to the instrument and the performer;" and running to his room, he came back with the harmonica, and held it up before the Baron—an oblong square, of the shape of a comb, the size of a small woman's hand, with twelve holes on each side of the breadth of it.

"Pleasanter to the ears than to the eyes," said the Baron, looking at it, "to be compared to a fine soul in a 'plain body.'"

Carlino played on it, and very cleverly, a Piedmontese air which pleased his master, but not half so much so as had done the simple chords with the long faint echoes which had struck home to his heart.

"So I have a musician in my service, and knew nothing of it. How was it that I never heard you play before?"

"I was not sure it would be agreeable to Monsieur."

"I understand—your master's temper was not the most encouraging to music. But I have turned over a new leaf, you know, and for the future, I shall be much obliged to you if you will give me the benefit of your harmonica whenever you feel so inclined. Have you had it long?"

"According to my reckoning, about fourteen years."

"Fourteen years count for something at your age. You must have been very young when you got it?"

"I was not quite eleven years old. I found it on the road between Aosta and Biella."

"You excite my curiosity: tell me all about it," said the Baron.

"Well, then," said Carlino, "I must begin by telling Monsieur how it was that we had to leave Bovino, and go to Aosta. We were five in family—father, mother, a girl, a boy, and I. Little Annette, the youngest, had died, when only eleven months old. My father was a muleteer, and went thrice a week to and from Biella, with his two mules. There was at that time no carriage road between Bovino and Biella. My sister, the eldest of us, and my brother, the second eldest, were employed at the cloth-mill. Ours was, and still is, a cloth-manufacturing district, and the most of our young people flocked for employment to the factory—a huge, naked building, all honeycombed with small windows, which stands at the end of the village, looking towards Biella. My occupation was to lead to pasture our two goats, and to take care of them otherwise. I suppose I was very young, or very small of my age, for I was not as tall as the goats. I was bid to keep them on a narrow strip of common, which bordered the road right and left, and on no account to let them stray beyond. I held to my orders, and executed them to the letter. If Monsieur had seen me, as I remember myself, a small, bareheaded, barefooted urchin, in a shirt and trousers too short even for me, held up only by one brace—if Monsieur had seen me in this accoutrement skipping after my goats, stick in hand, all day long, giving them and myself no rest, I am sure Monsieur would have warned me against zeal. Yes, zeal was my strength, or my weakness, as early as that, and will remain so to the end of the chapter. But I weary Monsieur——"

"Not at all, go on, you amuse me," said the Baron.

Carlino went on. "I remember the time when we were a happy, and, to all appearance, a prosperous family, when my mother used to sing all day, like a lark, at her work, when, on week-days, there was always plenty of maize bread and minestra, and on

Sundays a dish of salt pork and white bread was sure to be on the table—and when I had a nice suit of fustian and a good pair of shoes to go to mass in. But on a sudden all this changed; my mother continued to work, but sung no more, the salt pork and the white bread became things of the past, my nice suit of fustian went to tatters, my shoes fell off my feet with old age, and no new ones came to replace them. I know but vaguely the cause of this change. My father was an enterprising man, and fond of speculations, and having no capital he had to borrow money and to sign bills, which he could not take up. In short, we were ruined, and one fine day there was an execution in our house, and the house itself and all that was in it was knocked down to the best bidder; and then it was that my father, who was also a mason, made up his mind to go to Aosta, where he knew that workmen were needed for the building of some houses. My mother and I were to go with him, but not so my brother and sister, whose earnings at the cloth-mill were sufficient to keep them. They had been, however, so unhappy at the factory, their life there, ever since our misfortune, had been so full of humiliations, especially for my brother, that they begged hard to be allowed to join us, and they ended by getting my father to agree that they should go with us to Aosta. I must tell Monsieur that in our country to have one's house sold by law is looked upon as the height of disgrace. Most of the factory people shunned my sister; scarcely one of the girls would speak to my brother, not to mention the taunts and sneers which were their daily pittance. So the five of us went together to Aosta, on foot, of course, and found there well-paid employment for us all. I alone, for carrying sand and stones, earned as much as twenty sous a day; but as I was not strong, the sand and stones were too much for me, and I was soon on the sick list. I tried again and again, and always broke down. I was bitterly mortified; the more so as my father grumbled and scolded as though it had been my fault. I did nothing but cry. He had grown hard and stern to every one of us since he had become poor.

"He said one day, 'We cannot keep this boy here doing nothing while we work like cart-horses; he must go back to Bovino and try his chance at the factory. At his age his brother gained ten sous a day.' My mother prayed that I might remain a little longer, because of my weakness, but she prayed to no purpose. So one day, or rather one night, for it was at two in the morning, I was sent off. By making me start so early they had reckoned that I could reach Bovino on the morrow before nightfall. According to my father's directions, I was to apply to Giromè, a poor old neighbour of ours, for help and advice. Giromè had always been friendly to us, and had a son employed at the mill. I had also a letter from my sister to one of the best hands there, the one who was to be my brother-in-law, who had spoken to her for two years past. We say in our parts when a young man courts a girl that he speaks to her.

"It was in the month of July that I set out on my solitary journey—the moon was nearly full, the night as clear as day. My mother went with me a little way, then kissed me in a hurry (I guessed that she was afraid of my father), bade me be of good heart, put into my hand a little paper parcel, and was gone. There were in the packet three *mutte*, coins of the value of eight sous each—all her savings, I am sure. I never felt so miserable and lonely in my life as when she left me. I cried as though my heart would break. I was also stung by a feeling of shame, that I could not earn my bread as well as my brother and sister; but, in spite of my tears and my mortification, I kept on at a good pace. It might have been still a quicker one but for my old tattered shoes, one or other of which I was always losing; so, at last I took them off, and walked barefooted. At first it was quite a comfort, but here and there the road was so rough, so covered with stones, that after a while my feet got sore, and I had to put the shoes on again. It was a weary journey in every way. I stopped several times to rest and eat a bit of the maize bread I had in my pocket. I longed to sleep, but I dared not give way for fear of not getting to Bovino before night, so I did my best to resist the temptation. But when the sun rose high in the sky, and the midday heat was great, I suspect I must have taken a doze now and then, but only short ones.

"My anxiety to arrive before dark stood me in lieu of an alarm watch, and so on I trudged as well as I could, until my knees became so stiff that it was a serious affair to bend them; and I began to dread that I should not reach Bovino at all. My feet also were swollen, and blistered, and burning, and ached to such a degree that at last I could not bear it, and threw myself down under a tree by the roadside, and took off what remained of my shoes to cool my feet in the grass. As I did this, my right foot struck against something, which I saw was not a stone. I sat up and looked to see what this obstacle might be, and I found this harmonica in its case. I took it out. I had never seen anything of the kind before, nor, of course, did I know its name. I examined it narrowly, and perceiving the holes, instinctively put it to my lips. Oh! Monsieur, I can't tell you how transported I was with the sound I produced; it seemed to me as if somebody was speaking to me words of soothing and encouragement. I tried it again and again, and made it sound better and better. I no longer felt alone. I forgot my fatigue, though I had to remember it again when, after a long halt, I got up and strove to set forward once more. However, I found that walking was out of the question. Stand up I could, but not make one step forward; my knees wouldn't bend. I lay down again, and considered what I had best do. Consideration was of little use; if I could not move I must stay where I was till I could. So I rolled up my jacket, laid my head upon it, and fell asleep.

"I was roused by a voice calling to me. A gentleman on horseback had stopped in front of me. I must have slept long, for I felt quite refreshed, but my legs—in my bewilderment I had jumped up—my legs were as stiff and weak as ever. My head was so full of my newly-found treasure, that my first thought was that this gentleman must be the owner of it, and that he had come to ask for it. So I took it out of my pocket, and, showing it, said, 'Is this thing yours?'

"'No, how did you come by it?'

"'I found it lying here,' said I, pointing to the spot. 'May I keep it?'

"'Of course you may, if the rightful owner does not claim it. You must have come some distance, to judge from your feet.' I told him from whence I came, and where I was going, which led to further questions and answers, at the end of which the gentleman on horseback must have known as much about my affairs and those of my family as I did myself.

'I'm going to give you a lift to Bovino,' said the gentleman; 'can you manage to jump up to me?' I tried, but utterly failed; my knees were still too stiff. Seeing which he dismounted, lifted me on to the front of the saddle, then got up again himself, passed his arm round my waist, and away we started at a good canter. I was not a bit afraid, having ridden my father's mules many a time. We reached Bovino after dusk. I slipped off the horse in front of Giromè's cottage and thanked my benefactor to the best of my powers. He told me to stop a minute, wrote something in his pocket-book, tore out the leaf, and gave it to me, saying, 'Take that to the foreman of the cloth-mill, but I advise you to wash yourself well before you go to him, because you are very dirty, my poor boy.' And upon this he galloped away. I was indeed very dirty, and very much ashamed I was at his remark."

"The gentleman on horseback," said the Baron, "I guess was afterwards your master?"

"He was indeed, but I did not find out who he was until a week later, when he came to the factory. He stood by me some time watching me work—I was preparing spindles, the A B C of the craft—he praised my diligence, and desired me to go to his house at Biella the following Sunday. Of course I did not fail to do so. He seemed to like to hear me chatter in my childish way; he questioned me a good deal, among other things he inquired if I could read, and on my answering in the negative, said I ought to learn, and must do so. Meanwhile, I was living at Giromè's, taking my meals there and sleeping in the hayloft, and I made great friends with Giromè's son, a lad of fourteen, who knew how to read and write, and he volunteered to teach me. I was very proud on my next Sunday's visit to Signor Colletta, to show him that I knew my letters; he was much pleased at this, made me repeat them over and over again, and, in fact, became in some measure my teacher. At the end of a year I could read and write tolerably. I had also made some proficiency in my trade, and earned as much as fifteen sous a day. With that I could not only pay for my meals and washing at Giromè's, which I had been able to do for the last three quarters of a year, but also put by something. I had nothing to pay for lodging, as I continued to sleep in the hayloft, and as for clothes and linen, my kind protector had given me plenty of both, which Giromè's wife cut down to my size.

"As I grew older and cleverer, Signor Colletta seemed to take to me more and more. He would often speak confidentially to me, say, for instance, that he was weary to death of the cloth-mill and the cares it entailed upon him. In fact, he had not been bred up to be a man of business—the factory had devolved upon him quite unexpectedly through the sudden death of an elder brother. He was a man of studious and retired habits—a downright well of learning—always reading and talking about politics (all the liberals of the province looked up to him as their chief), and then so good and considerate. His patience with Marco, his deaf gruff servant, was truly angelic; and I was very often quite angry at Marco's want of attention and rough ways to his master. What would I not have given to be in Marco's place, to make the good Signor as comfortable as I could, and show him my gratitude for all he had done for me! This became my one wish, and grew with my growth.

"At last it was realised. Marco fell seriously ill, and Signor Colletta took me into the house. I nursed Marco, and did his work for more than a month. At last Marco recovered to a certain degree, but was too broken down to resume his service. Then it was that Signor Colletta, having handsomely provided for the old man, proposed to me to take Marco's place, and I need not tell Monsieur how happy I was to do so. I was just seventeen. At about the same time my master made over the management of the mill to his younger brother, the one who sent me to Paris. In 1847, the year of the Statuto, Signor Colletta was elected a Deputy, and I went with him when he went to Turin, to take his seat in the Chamber of Deputies. Two years later he was made Prefect at Chambery, and .... Monsieur knows the rest."

"And what became of the rest of your family?" asked the Baron.

"After a little more than a year's absence, my brother and sister went back to Bovino, and both resumed work at the mill. Some short time later my sister married the young workman who had courted her. My brother was taken by the conscription and became a soldier. My father settled at Aosta, opened a wine-shop, which proved a failure in the end, took to the mason's trade again, fell from a scaffolding, and was killed on the spot. My mother returned to Bovino, and lived with her daughter and son-in-law till 1849, when she went to Novara to nurse my poor brother, who had been badly wounded in the battle of that name, and was lying in the hospital. She came back to Bovino after his death, took to her bed, and in a very few days died. My sister and I are the only ones left of the family."

CHAPTER VII.

THIS day marked the beginning of a new era in the Baron's household. He never swerved for a moment from the programme which he had laid down for himself. His meekness and his serenity, even under acute suffering, never belied themselves. Let us hasten to add that God, in his mercy, was pleased to temper the wind to the shorn lamb; his fits of pain now occurred but seldom, and were as nothing in comparison to that dreadful attack at Divonne, the mere remembrance of which made Carlino's hair stand on end. The Baron, Carlino, and Victorine lived more like friends, or better still, more like members of the same family, than as master and servants, and a more united family it would not be easy to meet.

Little by little, the result of a gentle and continued pressure from Monsieur, it had become an established habit that Victorine, whenever unoccupied, should go and join her master in the study, his favourite room, and that, whether spoken to or not, there she should remain, an integrant part of the family circle, to which indeed she brought a precious accession of practical good sense and of keen observation. The long winter evenings, from six to nine, the Baron's hour for retiring, they as a rule spent together. Carlino or Victorine read aloud the evening newspapers and discussed the news; the Baron, if disposed, took a share in the conversation, and if not so inclined, bade them talk as if he were not present, contenting himself with listening. Then Carlino and Victorine occasionally played a game at cards or draughts, the various phases of which the invalid would follow with interest. At rare intervals, for continued talking fatigued him, he would relate to them some passages of his soldier's life in Africa. As nine struck, Carlino would take up his harmonica and sound the retreat, when Victorine disappeared, and Carlino wheeled his master into the bedroom.

Thus the first half of the winter wore on, monotonous, indeed, nay, often dull—how could it be otherwise?—but exempt from storms. About this time there arose a difficulty touching a certain payment which fell due to the Baron, and for which a receipt was demanded, that the poor gentleman was incapable of giving. Whereupon he sent for a notary and directed him to draw up a power of attorney, authorising Carlino to receive and give receipts for all rents, dividends, and moneys whatever appertaining to the Baron. This transaction brought to light the fact that the name Carlino, which every one who knew him, his master included, supposed to be a surname, was merely the diminutive of his Christian name Carlo, that of his family being Benvenuti. From this day Carlino received and made payments, kept the money and all the keys, and such was the Baron's implicit confidence in his servant's fidelity, that he was with difficulty persuaded to cast a cursory glance over the accounts, which every week Carlino submitted to his inspection.

On the morning of the day following that in which the power of attorney had been drawn up, the Baron said, while being dressed, "I think I ought to make my will; what do you say?"

"It is the sight of the notary which has put that

into Monsieur's head," returned Carlino; "why, there is no reason against doing so. My late master used to say that all rational beings, with property to dispose of, ought to make their wills at five-and-twenty; but of course, only if Monsieur has a wish to do so, for, thank God, there is no occasion for any hurry." Carlino was prompted to add this reservation by a shade of vexation which he had noticed, or fancied pass over his master's countenance. A long and close observation had given Carlino a keen perception of all the varieties of his master's feelings.

"You are mistaken," said the Baron, "if you suppose that the idea of making my will has anything unpleasant for me. If I could only believe, with many superstitious people, that doing so brings ill luck, as they say, I should seize on this chance of hastening my deliverance, and send for the notary at once. No; what perplexes me is that I have not yet settled in my mind how I shall dispose of my property."

"That is quite another matter," remarked Carlino, "and Monsieur can think, for nothing presses."

The Baron looked thoughtful throughout the whole day. He said suddenly that evening, when Carlino was putting him to bed, "You had a sister, had you not?"

"Yes, thank God, and still have her," answered Carlino.

"Then you are on friendly terms with her?"

"Friendly terms!" repeated Carlino, astonished; "surely, like brother and sister. I cannot say anything better."

"She is good?"

"As good as gold—excellent."

"You have never quarrelled with each other!"

"Never; we never had any reason for quarrelling. I cannot imagine any cause she could have given me, or I her."

"She is married, is she?"

"Yes, and has five children—three girls and two boys," said Carlino.

"Suppose she had married against your will?"

"It could not have happened, because, if she had persisted, I should have given way."

"Even if she had married a scamp?"

"My sister is not the sort of woman to marry a scamp, Monsieur."

"But supposing she had, what would you have done?"

"Well," said Carlino, after a little thought, "supposing she had—— I would have put up with it all the same, because I should have said to myself, as she has got this scamp, more need for me to help her and be kind to her."

"And suppose you had property to leave?"

"Why, if I had no wife nor children of my own, I should leave it to her and her children."

"In short, however badly your sister had behaved, you would never have found it in your heart to be angry with her?"

"I believe not," said Carlino.

The Baron mused a little, then said, "I wish I could feel as you do, Carlino. Yours, I have no doubt, is the right sort of feeling, but—— You are a noble-hearted fellow. I respect you."

After this the subject was never mooted again between them, but the sequel will soon show that the Baron argued the point with himself in the silence of his thoughts.

The beginning of spring coincided with an event which, much as it interested the public in general, was fraught with a still greater interest for our invalid. The section of railroad between Culoz and Chambery was opened, and thus the line of railway was uninterrupted between Chambery and Paris. The Baron's castle was therefore no longer inaccessible to him, for the few miles intervening between Chambery and the castle could be easily managed in a carriage. This enlargement of horizon, this unique chance of change was grasped at by the Baron with an eagerness, of which only a prisoner in a dungeon can form a somewhat adequate idea. The castle and everything connected with it, the mountains, the woods, the vines, his morbidly excited fancy invested with a poetic halo, which cast some of its rays even upon the remembrance of the old Vidame's anything but poetic figure. The mere thought of the gathering of the grapes, at which he had been present only two years ago, and had viewed with the most perfect indifference, save as to the quantity and quality of wine the vintage might produce, now brought tears to his eyes.

Carlino, to whom he immediately appealed, entered heart and soul into his master's wishes and anticipations, too happy that his thoughts should have a bright spot to alight and settle upon. "Down there," observed Carlino, "we shall have none of those thumps and shocks, which make the house tremble, and startle one out of one's sleep." To understand the force of this remark of Carlino's, it is necessary to bear in mind, that at the time he was speaking, the spring of 1856, there was already in full operation that systematic turning of Paris upside down, of which none to this day can foresee the end, and one of the least inconveniences of which was the exasperating awful noise created by the carting of building materials at every hour of the day and of the night. To this cause, though certainly not the only one, the Baron attributed the broken sleep from which he had suffered of late.

It was accordingly settled that he should leave

Paris as soon as the hot weather set in, earlier if possible, certainly not later than the first week of June. Carlino in the meantime was to see to the packing of the furniture and movables, it being the Baron's intention to give up his apartments, and quit Paris for good and all. All these arrangements were decided on *séance tenante*, that is, in the half-hour following the first mention of the change contemplated by the Baron. Victorine therefore knew nothing and could know nothing of the new projects. The Baron and Carlino had both of them taken it for granted that she would, as a matter of course, go with them. They had, however, reckoned without their host. No sooner did Carlino break the news to her than he perceived by her change of colour how unwelcome it was. How could she possibly forsake her old and infirm mother? It was out of the question. Carlino had not thought of this, and admitted the full force of the objection. Here was a sad complication which, if known to the Baron, would throw a damp on all his pleasure. What was to be done? At all events they must keep the truth from him for the present. Therefore it was agreed between them that Victorine should speak and act as though her being one of the party were an understood thing—then, when the moment of starting arrived, she must allege a sudden illness of her mother's, which forced her to remain behind for a few days. Thus time would be gained until Carlino should find a favourable opportunity for informing his master of the real state of the case. With what a heavy heart poor Carlino contrived this pious fraud, those who have observed his brotherly affection for Victorine, and the great assistance she had been to him in the care of his master, can easily guess.

April and May went by quick as lightning to Victorine's sad fore-knowledge, slow as a snail's pace to the Baron's impatience. The bulk of the furniture had been sent off a week ago; the weather was bright and warm as could be desired; in fact nothing more remained to do but to name the day of departure, and to bespeak a bed-carriage, and at last this also was done. Early on the second of June—they were to start at eight in the evening—Victorine was summoned to her mother's bed-side, such at least was the explanation given by Carlino to the Baron—an explanation confirmed in the course of the day by a letter from Victorine. She wrote that there was nothing serious in her mother's illness, but that such as it was it rendered it impossible for her to start just now. She begged Carlino to excuse her to her master, and to say that she hoped to join them in a few days at the castle. This assurance went far to lessen the Baron's disappointment.

At a little before six all the preparations were completed, and the herculean labour began. We have not the heart to dwell on the increase of infirmity and helplessness, which rendered the handling of the unfortunate gentleman a far more arduous task than on the previous occasion. He was besides much agitated at leaving Paris, and his home of many years, leaving them for ever, and the staring of all his neighbours was little calculated to allay that agitation. At last it was over, and he lay stretched on his travelling couch, panting, worn out already before starting. The wind created by the rush of the train revived him a little; but it soon became too much for him, and he complained of cold. The motion of the carriage harassed and made him restless; he had continually to beg that his posture might be changed. From Dijon to Macon the engine tore on at a furious, maddening pace, probably to make up for lost time—the train jerked from side to side as though striving to escape from the rails, and each jerk wrenched a groan of pain from the invalid. It was as if all his bones were being broken. Poor Carlino, half-wild with terror, but not the less self-possessed and indefatigable, never ceased administering cordials to his master, together with all the gentle words of cheering and consolation, that his long experience and his deep attachment could suggest, bitterly reproaching himself all the while for not having insisted on a physician being consulted before this journey had been undertaken.

By the time they reached Culoz the Baron was reduced to such a state of weakness as almost took away his power of speech, and it required a great effort for him to say to Carlino, during a few minutes' halt, "If we reach Chambery .... in safety, send for a notary directly—my uncle's notary, M. Giblat, to make my will. Do you promise?"

Carlino said he would send for M. Giblat as soon as the Baron had had some rest and was fit for business.

"No, no," insisted the Baron; "the notary first. I can have no rest till my will is made. God grant me time for that, or I shall die in despair."

"Monsieur's orders shall be obeyed; but Monsieur must not talk of dying," said Carlino, in the gentle tone of a mother chiding a wayward child. "A strong man like Monsieur does not die for so little. Monsieur wants rest, and must and shall have it, and then Monsieur will be himself again in no time. It is Carlino who says it, and knows it;" and as he thus spoke he wiped—oh, so tenderly—his master's forehead and face, all moist with drops of agony.

"Faithful heart!" murmured the sufferer. "Lay your hand on my head: it does me good."

As Carlino did so, the Baron closed his eyes, and gradually the muscles of his countenance relaxed. He no longer complained—nay, had, to all appearance, some snatches of sleep. Had the hand on his head anything to do with this interval of calm? Does such a thing as magnetic power, a mysterious physical influence of man over man, really exist? Many of those who have watched long by the sick-bed of one dearly loved, will answer in the affirmative. Carlino, be it remembered, at the time of his second journey to Paris, had found the Baron in a sharp fit of pain, and his presence had sufficed to cut it short. Be this as it may, Chambery was reached without much further discomfort.

"The notary, remember!" whispered the Baron, as he opened his eyes.

Madame Ferrolliet, informed beforehand of the day and hour of their arrival, was waiting at the terminus with a carriage full of pillows and warm coverings, and with the whole of her household in attendance. Carlino went to her and explained, in as few words as possible, the state of the case, and the urgent necessity for a notary and a physician. Madame Ferrolliet sent off one of her servants in search of M. Giblat, and of the first medical man of the town; then, approaching the carriage where the Baron lay, welcomed him to Chambery and her house, begging him at the same time not to tire himself by answering her. Carlino and the servants of Madame Ferrolliet carefully raised the Baron in their arms and gently transferred him to the carriage; but such was his exhaustion that, in spite of all their care and gentleness, he fainted away. Bent double and unconscious, an object of pity to all lookers on, Baron Gaston de Kerdiat was carried through the gate of the Hôtel de l'Europe, that gate which of yore he had so often passed, full of life and strength, stiff, haughty, almost threatening. No one who had known him at that time could have identified in the shrunken, aged looking form of to-day the powerfully built man in the prime of manhood of two years ago.

Madame Ferrolliet had got ready for her guest two rooms on the ground-floor, her own two rooms, and thither he was carried, put into a warm bed, rubbed with hot flannels, supplied, in short, with all the restoratives that art can devise. After ten minutes, or so, these efforts were successful; he heaved a deep sigh, opened his eyes, gazed around with a scared look, which changed to one of satisfaction the moment he caught sight of the familiar face of his uncle's notary. "Ah, Monsieur Giblat!" he gasped forth, in a voice scarcely audible, "Thank God!"

"Monsieur," here interposed a gentleman in black, who all this while had been examining the sick man's pulse, "Monsieur, we shall leave you with Monsieur Giblat as soon as you have swallowed a potion which I have prescribed, and which is being prepared for you. I can assure you there is no cause for alarm, you are merely exhausted by your journey, and want nothing but rest and nourishment."

"Thank you," said the Baron, and his eyes just then meeting those of Madame Ferrolliet, he added,

"Dear Madame, how can I ever enough apologise for the trouble I am giving you? God bless you! It is my sad privilege to reap nothing but kindness where I sowed only harshness."

Two big tears that rolled down her cheeks were all the answer that the good lady could make. The kind doctor here saw fit to interfere. "Allow me to warn you, my dear sir, against giving way to emotion; it tends to weaken you. Madame Ferrolliet will not contradict me when I say that she is but too happy to be of some service to an old and honoured customer of her house, and we are all of us happy to be of use to you. Here comes my potion, my elixir of long life, I call it; drink it, sir, and you will wonder at the feeling of comfort which will afterwards pervade all your being."

The Baron drank it. "Now," added the doctor, "we will leave you to a *tête-à-tête* with your notary," and he left the room, followed by all excepting M. Giblat and Carlino. Carlino looked inquiringly at his master, who in answer slightly nodded in the direction of the door, and Carlino went away.

The interview was short. At the end of twenty minutes M. Giblat came out of the room, and Carlino went in. "How does Monsieur feel?" asked he.

"Much better," replied the Baron; "that potion of the doctor's did me a great deal of good."

"God be thanked," said Carlino.

"I wish to explain to you," resumed the Baron, "why I banished you just now. I have put you down in my will for a trifle, and it would be contrary to law that you should witness my doing so."

Quickly rising tears filled Carlino's eyes; he said, in a husky voice, "I hope Monsieur believes that what I do for him is out of deep love and duty, and not at all from any interested motives."

"I am fully convinced of your affection, my good Carlino. Service for hire differs widely from service for love."

Here there was a knock at the door, and Madame Ferrolliet came in on tiptoe with a steaming cup in her hand. "Only a sprinkle of vermicelli in a cup of *consommé*, that I have made myself for you, Monsieur le Baron, will you try it?"

"Certainly," said the Baron; "all that comes from your hands must be good and welcome." She fed him with spoonful after spoonful of the *potage* till he had swallowed it all, wiped his mouth with a napkin, and then quietly withdrew. "Kind soul!" exclaimed the Baron; "I owe to my misfortune the discovery of mines of goodness and worth where I suspected none. Too late, alas! for me to act upon this newly-acquired knowledge—too late!" He shut his eyes, and might have been thought asleep, but that the motion of his lips testified that he was praying.

Some time later M. Giblat returned, accompanied by a brother official, and followed by a string of witnesses. Carlino counted seven of them. He ushered them into his master's room, and retired. The writing out of the will took a little more than an hour. As the notaries and the witnesses passed through the ante-room where Carlino was waiting, M. Giblat accosted him, saying, "You are M. Carlino, the Baron de Kerdiat's confidential servant?"

"I am," replied Carlino.

"This, then, is for you," returned M. Giblat, handing him a paper. "It contains some of the last wishes of the Baron, of which he has desired that you should now have a copy. You are to break the seal only in the event of his death. Allow me at the same time," continued M. Giblat, in quite another tone, "to avail myself of this opportunity to express to you in my own name and that of my colleague, and all the gentlemen present, our respect for the unparalleled devotion you have displayed in Monsieur le Baron's service."

Carlino, red as a cock's comb up to the very roots of his hair, bowed low, and hastened to his master. He found him as white as the sheet which covered him, but with a placid face.

"I am so thankful to have been in time," he said. "Did Monsieur Giblat give you a paper?" Carlino made an affirmative sign. "All right. By-and-by I will tell you something that will give you pleasure. I require rest now, and you also, my poor Carlino."

"We will, please God, have a sound sleep, and not wake before to-morrow morning," rejoined Carlino, cheerfully; "but first Monsieur must take the drink that Madame Ferrolliet is bringing him." The Baron did so, with many thanks to Madame. "Monsieur has no need to rouse himself," added Carlino, "when from time to time I give him a spoonful from this bottle. It is the same potion which has already done Monsieur so much good."

"I will swallow it as in a dream," said the Baron. Carlino brought in a mattress, placed it by the side of the bed, arranged his master's pillows and bed-clothes, closed the blinds, and then laid himself down. It was then six o'clock in the afternoon. The Baron slept, to all appearance soundly, and did but half wake when Carlino, in obedience to the doctor's prescription, every half hour put a spoonful of the cordial into his mouth. At a little after midnight the patient awoke fully, and said suddenly, "Carlino, did I ever tell you that I had a sister?"

"No, sir—is she dead?"

"She has been the same as dead to me for these last ten years. She married against my will, married a man for love, to whom I had an objection, and we have been strangers to each other ever since."

"Oh, what a misfortune!" said Carlino; "the man

Monsieur's sister married was, then, a disreputable character?"

"No; everybody who knew him gave him a high character, as being clever and honest; but he was of another class from her, he was of low birth, the son of a farmer, and was himself only a village schoolmaster; and that was why I objected to him."

"But if he was clever and good, and likely to make the lady happy, it would not much matter, would it, Monsieur, whether he was lowly or highly born?" said Carlino, sagaciously nodding his head.

"I was very proud—proud of the race from which we sprung, and I considered a *mésalliance* as the greatest possible disgrace. Pride has been the bane of my life. In breaking off all intercourse with my sister, I believed I was only fulfilling a duty. I began not to be quite so clear as to that after a conversation I had with you in reference to your sister. At that moment I was for the first time thinking of making my will, and debating with myself whether I should be justified in benefiting some stranger by the exclusion of my sister. In short, the seed you had sown in my mind during the conversation to which I allude, never ceased growing until it bore fruit. You will be glad to hear that in the will I have made to-day, I have left my sister the bulk of my fortune—a result for which she may well be thankful to you."

"Rather say to Monsieur's just and kind heart," exclaimed Carlino, with a gush of feeling. "And Monsieur forgives her?"

"I do fully," said Baron Gaston. "I stand more in need of her pardon than she of mine, for she was always kind to me while I was very harsh to her." And here he told Carlino of that most affectionate letter which he had received from his sister shortly after his accident, and of the scornful silence with which he had treated it.

"Reason the more," said Carlino, "why Monsieur should not lose a moment in acknowledging to her that he did wrong, and in sending her his love and blessing. What is the lady's name? Where does she live?"

"Her name is Madame Marie Moron, and her letter was dated from Le Mans."

"Shall I write and invite her to come to Monsieur at the Castle?"

"Not just now. I feel that the emotion of such a meeting would be too much for me."

"At all events, Monsieur will permit me to write to her an account of the conversation we have just had?"

"Yes, you may do so," said the Baron.

He looked rather drowsy, and his utterance had become somewhat thick and embarrassed; thereupon Carlino hid the night-light and begged his master to try and sleep again.

He tried, but with little success, as shown by the

frequent mutterings to which he gave way, and the only distinct words that could be heard was the oft-repeated name of Divonne. Perhaps he was dreaming, and in that case it would be a pity to wake him. Carlino sat up, and listened long, much perplexed what to do, until his uneasiness got the better of his unwillingness to run the risk of interrupting his master's slumbers. He stood by the bedside and asked, "Are you in pain, sir?"

"Quite the contrary," was the reply. "I have not felt as comfortable for a long while. I feel as light as a feather! What o'clock is it?"

"Nearly three in the morning."

"Suppose you order a carriage and let us start for the Castle at eight?"

"Certainly," said Carlino, humouring the Baron's notion. "We'll see the doctor though, first. Monsieur must have been dreaming about Divonne."

"So I was. A glorious place that Divonne! Do you remember that girl who could not even sit up? I wonder what has become of her."

"Let us hope that she is better," answered Carlino.

A long pause ensued.

"Where is your harmonica?" asked the Baron, all at once.

"I have it here, sir."

"Play on it a little, will you? It will put me to sleep."

Carlino took up his little instrument and played some chords.

"Delicious!" muttered the Baron. "It is like music from heaven. Sleep steals softly on me. Good night, Carlino."

"Good-night, dear master."

"And friend," prompted the Baron, in a scarcely audible whisper.

"And friend," repeated Carlino.

The incipient dawn was tinging with whitish grey the interstices of the bars of the closed blinds, and imparting to the air a pleasant freshness. It was that mysterious hour of universal appeasement, when even the anxious and the sick lay down their load for a while, and find rest. Carlino felt the influence of the hour, and though with reluctance, succumbed to it. He had not shut his eyes for the last forty-eight hours, and tired nature asserted her rights. He fell into profound sleep, which, however, did not last long, not so long as an hour. He awakened with a sense of remorse, as of one who had deserted his post. He raised himself first on his elbow, as was his wont, and listened. No sound whatever. He went to the bed, bent over his master's lips—no breath issued from them—he felt his forehead—cold as ice. Carlino rung the bell furiously to alarm the house. Every one hurried to the room, the doctor was sent for, everything was done that could be done to restore animation, but in vain. Baron Gaston de Kerdiat had laid down his burden for ever.

Carlino soon found out, to his great surprise, that of all the persons who had approached his master, he was the only one not prepared for this fatal result. The physician from the first had looked upon the Baron as dying—a too well-founded conclusion, of which, in his own justification, he had made a mystery to no one, except to the faithful servant: we say in his own justification, for had the doctor perceived any the least glimpse of hope, he would have been inexcusable in allowing his patient to be fatigued by notaries and testamentary arrangements. Yet even the physician did not expect so rapid an end.

After the first uncontrollable burst of grief, Carlino bethought himself that there still remained duties for him to perform, and that to perform them properly he must be composed. His first care was to telegraph to Madame Moron, and to make himself acquainted with the contents of the paper confided to him by Monsieur Giblat. These were its contents:—

"When it shall please God to call me to Him, I beg of my faithful servant and dear friend, Carlo Benvenuti, to give me a last proof of attachment by never leaving my body until it is consigned to the earth.

"I wish to be buried in the Cemetery of Chambery, as near as possible to the grave of my uncle, the Vidame de Kerdiat. I wish the Church service in behalf of my soul, and also my funeral, to be of the simplest, nay, of the humblest. No *lettres de faire part*, no music, no pomp whatever, no epitaph, no inscription of name or rank, to mark the spot where my bones lie, nothing save a small cross of marble.

"On the day *after* my burial I wish two thousand francs to be distributed among the poor of the place where I shall have died.

"I recommend the strict accomplishment of these my last wishes to the known piety and affection of the above-named Carlo Benvenuti, my faithful servant and dear friend."

Carlino conformed strictly to the spirit and the letter of these directions. The only departure from them which he allowed, or rather had no control over it, was the great affluence of persons who followed the body to the cemetery. In the absence of Madame Moron, Carlino, as a matter of course, was chief mourner.

Monsieur and Madame Moron arrived on the day following the funeral. The telegram had missed them at Le Mans, which they had left ten months previously, and in following them to Amiens, their new abode, had lost a day. Carlino gave them a faithful account of the conversation which had passed between his master and himself in reference to Madame Moron—an account with what emotion given, with what emotion received, I leave to the reader's heart to determine.

The opening of the deceased's will took place on the day week after the funeral. In the interval the Morons and Carlino had been much together, and had become quite friends. The Baron left to his sister the whole of his fortune, save a sum of eighty thousand francs, nominal value, in Piedmontese bonds, bequeathed to Carlino. The clause containing this legacy was worded thus:—

"To my faithful servant, and dear friend, Carlo Benvenuti, to whose attachment and devotion I am indebted not only for all the physical and moral comfort of which my illness admitted, but also for much evil avoided, and for a little good done, I leave and bequeath for his sole use and benefit the sum of," &c., &c.

Carlino's legacy amounted to nearly the fourth part of the Baron's whole fortune.

Carlino had lost no time in letting Victorine know of his master's death, and now he wrote again to tell her of the Baron's liberality, adding—"I know from our late master's lips that it was his intention to provide for you in a permanent manner, and I am only acting up to his wishes and to my own conscience when I assure you that you will receive a thousand francs yearly so long as you live."

Writing on the same subject to Beata, his affianced

bride, he said—"And so here we are possessors of a large fortune—large, I mean, in proportion to anything we could ever have expected in the natural course of things, and we must put our heads together to find out what best to do with it. The money has come to us through suffering and sorrow, and it is but justice that some of it should return to the sorrowful and the suffering. I have often thought what a blessing it would be to our folks at Bovino if, instead of being packed off when sick to the hospital at Biella, a two hours' journey, they had a place to go to in the village itself, where they could in the first instance receive some medical assistance—only a small place, a couple of beds to begin with. That surely would not cost much in our parts. Nurses we should not want—you and I would be more than enough. The great difficulty would be to find a good physician to help, but we may trust to God to help us. Think on it; I know you are willing."

The modest cross of marble being by this time laid on the Baron's resting-place, and the Morons gone to the Castle, nothing more remained for Carlino to do than to bid an affectionate farewell to Madame Ferrolliet, and to all his other old and new friends, and to set off for his beloved country, where we wish him success in his benevolent scheme, and all manner of happiness.

END OF "CARLINO."

A CONTEMPORARY HOBBY.

A CONTEMPORARY HOBBY.

I don't know how it fares with you in London, but I know that we in Paris have a sorry life of it. By which *it* I do not allude to the frost, nor to the macadamized Boulevards, nor to the tightness of the money-market—no, nor yet to the indefinite rise of house-rents, but to a far worse nuisance—the cardomania. Ever since it has become the fashion to have squinting, ghastly photographs, instead of the true, plain, honest visiting-card—ever since it has become the fashion to make collections of these said photographs—above all, ever since the fatal invention of albums *ad hoc*, farewell peace! Whichever way you turn, requests for your portrait are levelled at you like so many guns. All is acceptable prey; indifferent features, respectable age, obscure position—nothing comes amiss to that greedy monster, Album.

I give myself as an example. I, socially speaking, one of the most insignificant beings in creation, had so many home-thrusts to parry of late, that at last I was thrown out of the saddle. A lady did that for me—a clever and accomplished blonde—beware of blondes. She was doing me the honours of her album, and I was on the defensive. We came to an empty niche. She said pleasantly, calmly, decidedly, "That is for you." I did all a man can do—very little, I allow, when the adversary is one like my softly determined, smilingly implacable hostess—I laughed outright, found the joke excellent; then I became serious. She knew my habits—my dislike of all that makes a man a plaything, and so on. Grave or gay, it mattered not. Let the fair sex alone for holding to the point when it suits them.

"If, by New Year's Day," said the lady, "this niche is not filled by your photograph, I shall have been mistaken in your gallantry." I protested in favour of my gallantry; but surely she would grant me a respite, considering that just at that moment I was very busy—in all truth, overworked . . . .

"Oh, sir," was the quick rejoinder, "if I were asking for a miniature, even for a sketch in crayons; but a photograph! a sacrifice of five minutes!"

Whatever my misgivings about the five minutes, we live, as everybody knows, in a chivalrous age, and, to use the words of a great man, I am a man of my times. So I bowed my head, whispered something about wishes being commands, and went my way. My last thought on going to sleep that night, my first thought on awakening next morning, was that I must go and have my photograph done.

When a tooth must come out, the sooner it is out the better. In compliance with this wise aphorism, I sallied forth in quest of a—I was going to say "dentist"—in quest of a photographer. No need to go far; every second door on the Boulevard boasted the name of one. Next to literature, photography seems to be the favourite vocation of those who have none. Let me see. Mr. Perlet, *chimiste photographe*. Too much by half. I shall have to pay for the chemistry. Mr. Perlet shall not have my custom.

Messrs. Verplick Candish. This sounds outlandish, but safer;—a first-rate establishment—at least, if one may judge by the outside. Behold a richly-carpeted staircase, a banister of gilt and red velvet with coloured crystal globes at intervals, red velvet *portière* concealing the sanctuary to which the gorgeous ascent led!—Who pays for all this finery? Never mind. I shall do my blonde friend's behest handsomely.

So up I went, and, raising the crimson drapery, entered an ante-room, midway of which I was met by a fashionably-dressed gentleman, who asked if I had come for *cartes de visite*. I replied, "Exactly so; for *cartes de visite*." "Very well. Would I give myself the trouble to walk this way?" and the well-dressed gentleman passed behind a railed desk, while I took up a position in front of it. A voluminous ledger lay open on the desk.

"Will Monsieur give his name?"

As I had come for a portrait, and not for a passport, the request sounded strangely; nevertheless, I complied. Whatever may be my objection to giving my portrait, I have none against giving my name.

"Monsieur lives?" I said where I lived, and my address was added to my name.

"Monsieur has number 309," explained the gentleman; "Monsieur will be informed by letter of the day on which his turn comes."

"And when is my turn likely to come?" asked I.

"Impossible to fix a date; much depends on the weather, and other circumstances over which we have no control. I should say, in a month—perhaps even in three weeks."

"In that case, have the goodness to efface my name," said I; "I must have my cards on the last of the month at the latest."

The gentleman was sorry; but at this time of the year ... The whole person of the speaker, eyes, eyebrows, shoulders, hands, were eloquent in protestation of the vanity of my wishes. So without further parley I bowed myself out.

I spent a full hour in new trials; and, believe it or not, fair reader, but I say only the truth when I say that nowhere, either for love or money, could I get the promise of a photograph of myself, under fifteen days. Now, as it was already the 18th of December, and my card fell due on New-Year's day, a fortnight's delay placed me in the physical impossibility of keeping my word.

My best course was to quit the more aristocratic daily lounges, and try some less frequented neighbourhood, which possibly the fashionable epidemic had not yet attacked. With this hope I repaired to the Palais Royal. Here again there was too much of a good thing—rows and rows of photographs, and photographers' signboards stared at me from every corner. Like Yorick in search of a passenger from whom he might ask his way, I scanned the outward features of perhaps a dozen establishments, without seeing aught that could influence my choice one way or the other. At last I perceived this N. B. attached to a photographer's name. "Up at the seventh story." Eureka! cried I; no danger of competition from the lame and asthmatic here,—and up I climbed. I was received by a lady. I took it as a good omen. Women are more easy and pleasant to deal with than men. "Madame," said I, as soon as I could recover my breath, "I wish to have some *cartes de visite* done."

"Certainly," replied the lady, "how many do you...?"

"Excuse my interrupting you," I continued, in an unsteady tone, "but I should like to know how soon you can take my likeness."

"Immediately, if it suits you—(I could have hugged

the speaker to my bosom for these blessed words)—
that is," pursued she, "should the light serve, which I
rather doubt—really, we have no afternoon. At all
events, I will go and inquire of my husband."

Alas! the light, such light as it was, December
light, you remember, did no longer serve. Such was
the fiat with which the lady emerged from the glazed
door of an adjoining closet, evidently the photographer's workshop. But, if I would return on the
morrow about midday, I might make sure of having
my photograph taken.

Upon this understanding we parted. It was half-
past three when I reached home, and I had gone out
at half-past eleven. This preparatory work had cost
me four hours. I should have liked to ask my blonde
to reckon up how many *five minutes* there are in four
hours.

I was punctual to my rendezvous, next morning.
At three minutes to twelve by the time-piece of my
photographer (to be), I had taken up a position in
the lilliputian waiting-room. I saw with infinite
pleasure only a lady with two children here besides
myself. So far all right. Allowing an hour and a
half—I meant to be generous—for the sitting of my
fair competitor, and her small fry—a half hour apiece
—I stood a good chance of release by two o'clock.

But I had reckoned without the person then
actually being photographed, and this error I dis-

covered to my cost when all the clocks of the Palais Royal struck one, without bringing any alteration in the *status quo*. My partner in misfortune and I exchanged now and then glances of condolence and uttered sympathetic sighs. To add to our discomfort, the supply of fuel in the stove had been long exhausted, and the temperature of the waiting-room was gradually sinking.

"I am so cold, Mamma," exclaimed the little boy. Maternal love prompted a violent attack on the bell, which brought about a crisis. An immediate slamming of doors responded to the appeal of the bell, and in rushed simultaneously the photographer, his wife, and her maid. A short explanation or remonstrance ensued, the practical upshot of which was that mother and children were introduced into the sancta sanctorum, and the maid relighted the stove, cramming it with coals, to make sure, I suppose, of not being called on again to perform that duty.

Now this stove had a powerful draught, which set the coals in a blaze in no time; and, the waiting-room being extremely small, as I said, it presently grew so hot and close, that before the end of half an hour I wished the stove had been left alone. I would have opened the single window, but in front of it stood a table loaded with casts, stereoscopes, and other appurtenances of a photographer, which put it out of my power to reach the window. By way of diversion,

I tried the small passage leading to the stairs, but it was so chilly, and I was in such a heat, that, afraid of catching cold, I was obliged to content myself with taking up a position as far from the hissing furnace as the lilliputian proportions of the room allowed, puffing and panting for release.

It came at last, after forty-seven minutes' endurance of this temporary purgatory. The mother and children departed, and I took their place in the atelier; a happy first moment that was, when my foot crossed the threshold.

"Very poor light," observed the artist, by way of salutation. "Let us make the most of it as it is, by looking sharp," said L. The man being apparently of my opinion, a few seconds were enough for him to suggest, and for me to assume a becoming attitude in front of the four cannon-like tubes which were to reproduce my respected person four times at once. "We are going to begin—perfect immobility, if you please; keep your eyes steadily on the handle of the door; there." The operation began, and was done, or not done, in less than five minutes. So far my fair-haired lady was right.

The operator then disappeared with the plate into his laboratory, I saluting his exit with a volley of sneezes. The fact was, I had passed suddenly from the tropics to the arctic regions—the atelier being a sort of glass cage, open to all the winds of heaven, without a spark of fire. I hastened to don my overcoat, my hat, and comforter; thus prepared for departure, I waited to hear the result of the operation.

In course of time, the photographer re-appeared. "*Manqué*," said he, with a rueful face. "*Manqué*," was I going to repeat, in consternation, but the word was cut in two by another explosion of sneezes. "In all my experience I never saw such another abominable day for light," exclaimed the photographer. "However," he added, "suppose we try again." "Let us try again," said I; "is there any reason against my keeping on my hat and greatcoat? I am half frozen." "It would be a certain failure if I did so," was the answer; and so I had to part with my hat and upper garment, and sit in the draught unprotected.

Had the sacrifice only availed! but, no, the second attempt was not more fortunate than the first. "It was enough to drive a man crazy," declared the perplexed artist, "all had come out beautifully, but no head! Useless to make any more attempts that day. Would I call again on the morrow, before noon." Of course I would; I had no choice but to do so.

The loss of three hours, and the acquisition of a well-conditioned cold—such was the net balance of my second day's trial. Really if ladies, stung by the mania of making collections of photographs, knew to what they exposed their acquaintances, they would be a little more careful, thought I.

Contrary to my anticipations, which were of the blackest, everything on the morrow went as smooth as oil. I had to wait comparatively but a short time; the light was tolerably favourable, and the likeness—so, at least, averred the photographer—had come out capitally. He promised that my *cartes de visite* should be sent to me on the 26th (it was then the 20th); I left a card with my address, and went home to nurse my cold in peace, thankful at heart at having got rid of my incubus on such easy terms.

The 26th came and went; and so did the 27th; and heaven knows how many more days might have come and gone without my giving a thought to the *cartes de visite*, for I happened to be very busy at that time, had not chance thrown me on the evening of the 28th in the way of my fair persecutress of the "five minutes" at the house of a common friend. Of course, the sight of her would have been sufficient to recal to my mind my *cartes de visite*, even had she not chosen to remind me pointedly of my engagement, by playfully saying,—

"Remember that I am your creditor, and a very unmerciful one."

I said, rather tartly, I hoped not to put her powers of endurance to too severe a test, it being one among my few virtues to pay my bills punctually, and bowed low.

The first thing I did the next morning was to go and see after these blessed cards.

"Madam," said I to the lady, in whom I had seen a benignant influence on my first visit to the Photographer of the Palais Royal, "as you have not kept your promise of sending me my *cartes de visite*, I have come for them myself."

"Your cards, sir?" replied the lady, evidently perplexed; "dear me, then you have not received my letter."

"I have received no letter," said I.

"Then you are ignorant of the accident which has happened."

"Accident? what accident?" cried I.

"Perhaps Monsieur does not know that we use glass, as more sensitive to light than metal, though less safe. Well, your glass, I am pained to the heart to say, somehow or other, was thrown down, and shivered into atoms."

I was literally struck dumb by this unexpected catastrophe. I gave a deep groan. The lady continued,—

"I did not lose a minute in writing to you. I am sure I made no mistake, for" (fixing her eyes on me) "you are Mr. Wolf, are you not?"

("Mr. Wolf!!!")

"You live in the Rue des trois Epées?"

("Rue des trois Epées!!!")

"I copied the address from the card you left us. Where has it got to?" searching among several which were stuck in the frame of the mirror. "Ah! here it is; I knew I was right."

I cast my eyes on the card she presented to me, and read, "Mr. Wolf, Pedicure, 70, Rue des trois Epées." It wanted but this. To have to begin *ab ovo*, and to pass for a Pedicure into the bargain!

The lady was right; alas! the mistake was entirely my own. Let not this candid admission, impartial reader, cool your sympathy in my behalf; for, had nobody asked for my likeness, I should have had no occasion to go to a photographer; and, if I had not gone to a photographer, there would have been no ridiculous, soul-vexing mistake. The fact was, as I explained to the lady, that I had a—I beg your pardon—a corn, which made me suffer martyrdom. One of my friends advised me to apply to an excellent pedicure, whose address he would send. He sent it; and, as my evil star would have it, his note, inclosing Mr. Wolf's card, was delivered to me by my *concierge* just as I was going out on my third photographic expedition of the 20th. I put the card into my waistcoat pocket, and inadvertently gave it to the photographer instead of one of my own.

I had cause to be thankful that I was yet in time to repair my blunder.

"Madam," said I, with as much pathos as I could put in my voice, "I am pledged to give my *carte de visite* on New-Year's day; pray, madam, help me to do so. Name any price you think proper, but let me have my card."

"My dear sir," replied the lady, "be convinced that I feel for you; indeed I do; but you ask an impossibility. We are literally sinking under the weight of work; my husband is positively made ill by it. We had to refuse a good half of the applicants for cards, and—I would not own as much to anybody else, but really your situation distresses me—and even of those we have accepted, we shall be obliged to disappoint the greater number. Just take a peep into the waiting-room, will you? Full as an egg (and so it was). You see I speak the truth; why should I not? It is our interest to please the public——"

I stopped her to ask if she could point out any other photographer with whom I might have a chance of success. She said that, short of a miracle, she believed I had no chance anywhere. And upon this hopeful assurance I took my leave.

I had no particular reason to reckon on a miracle in my favour; besides my time was too short to allow my wasting any particle of it in what I was forewarned would be a useless search. A moment of reflection convinced me that there was but one course left for me to try. I beckoned to a cab, drove home, packed my carpet-bag, drove to the Strasburg Railway terminus, and took a ticket for Bar-le-Duc.

Why for Bar-le-Duc? Because of all the places on this terraquean globe Bar-le-Duc was the only one where I had a fair prospect of having my photograph done,—in other words, because there resided at Bar-le-Duc a friend of mine, who was an *amateur* photographer, and on whose assistance, if alive and capable, I knew I could rely.

You recollect the sort of weather which graced our latitude on the 29th December, 1860? If you don't, I do; wind, hail, snow, rain, and frost. My journey was a most abominable one. Twice we were detained by the snow: we reached our destination three hours after our time: it was midnight; too late to go to my friend's house, so I stopped at the first inn I came to—a most wretched hole it proved. Nothing hot to be had; a bed icy cold; and no sooner had I laid myself down than the fire went out. I groped in the dark (I had no matches with me) in search of a bellrope; I found none. I called out at the top of my voice,—my cries were unheard or unheeded. I could not shut my eyes for the cold. An icicle, as I had lain down overnight, an icicle I got up in the morning,—a bleak, funereal morning. It was snowing as thick and fast as though it had not snowed all night. Roofs and streets looked as if strewed with white sheets. Bar-le-Duc might have sat for Tobolsk.

If ever a man was surprised at the sight of another, it was my friend at sight of me. "Just like me," he declared, "he never——"

I hastened to explain the cause and object of my present visit.

"But, my dear friend," he objected, "you could not have chosen a more unfavourable moment."

"Did I say that I had chosen it? A bit of straw driven by the wind is not more passive than I am in this affair."

"With the snow falling in this way," he pursued, "no hope of doing anything tolerable."

"Let it, then, be something intolerable," said I.

"Really, you are not in a fit condition to have your likeness taken; you want rest. Go to the glass, and judge for yourself. You look like a ghost."

"Ghost or scarecrow, it does not matter; only for pity's sake take a photograph of me at once. I must be in Paris to-night; I have a paper to finish, and to send off by to-morrow's post."

Satisfied that he had done all in his power to enforce the claims of Art, always foremost in his eyes, my friend, in spite of the snow still falling, and the false light, undertook with a good grace the task I demanded of him. It required all his skill and patience to bring it to a plausible conclusion. The likeness obtained after two hours' hard work, bad as it was, he pronounced to be as good as could be hoped for under the circumstances. It was far from a flattering resemblance certainly, but for that I little cared. I should without fail receive a copy by post, on New Year's-day. I might rely on his punctuality; thereupon, with heartfelt thanks, I departed.

The same gentle influences which had accompanied me from Paris to Bar-le-Duc—snow, wind, cold, etc., etc.—favoured my return to Paris. I reached home more dead than alive. I tried hard to finish the paper I had engaged should be forwarded on the morrow, but in vain; I had to send instead an apology, which brought me in due course a good blowing up from the disappointed editor—one of the many perquisites of the trade.

The next day—the last of the year—was, I sincerely believe, one of the most uncomfortable days of my life. Dire anxiety weighed on every hour of it. Do what I would, I could not bring myself to believe that the card from Bar-le-Duc would arrive on the morrow. Something must happen to it. What had occurred before might occur again; nay, possibly it was quite in the ordinary course of photographic events that the plate or glass should break, or, if the photograph was sent, it might be smashed by a railway accident, or the envelope containing it be dropped by some careless postman. Anything seemed more likely than that it should arrive safely.

It did, though, to my inexpressible relief, and I hastened to carry it myself to its destination. The fair lady was from home; so I left it, carefully wrapped up, and addressed, with her *concierge;* and then, for the first time for fourteen days, I breathed freely.

In the evening I received the following note:—

"I regret very much to have missed seeing you this morning. Thank you for your card. It does not entirely satisfy me. You know I am extremely particular about my photographs; so do not be surprised should I ask you for the sacrifice of another five minutes. We will speak of that. Come and take a family dinner with us to-morrow, at half-past six. Mr. Paul, and Mme. Lorry, will be our only other guests. By the bye, they both think your likeness good, and mean each of them to beg you for one. So, be amiable enough to bring some more of your *cartes de visite* with you. *A demain donc.* Believe me, sans adieu.

"Yours sincerely,

"————."

The perusal of this note threw me into despair. And so, all the wear and tear of mind and body, all my loss of time, all my disbursements, were to go for nothing! to leave me at the point from which I had started! the stone I had lifted in the sweat of my brow recoiled on me! I took up the pen *ab irato* to say—what?—anything but that I accepted the invitation—to say that I was ill, that I had been called away by a telegram, that—that—but of what avail any excuse? To procure me a respite of a week —say of a month, and then? Why, all the botheration would have to be gone through anew. No, there was nothing for it. To go and settle in the backwoods of America, or to take the world as it was, hobbies included, such was the dilemma which rose before me, clear and defined; there was no escape. It was for me to choose. I pondered long, pen in hand, and then wrote this answer:—

"Dear Madam,—I accept with thanks your kind invitation for to-morrow. I regret that my *carte de visite* does not meet with your approbation; however, I am at your service for any number of experiments in the same line—in fact, until the result shall satisfy you. I am much flattered by the wish expressed by Mme. Lorry and Mr. Paul. I have written for an immediate supply of half-a-hundred copies of my card to meet the requests of my friends.

"Believe me, dear Madam,
"Ever yours, sincerely obliged,
"———."

END OF "A CONTEMPORARY HOBBY."

SANREMO REVISITED.

1857 - 1864

SANREMO REVISITED.

PART I.

Happening last autumn to make a short stay in the Riviera, one of my first thoughts was to go and pay a visit to Sanremo. I never fail to do so when I am in the neighbourhood.

I am very fond of Sanremo. I hope you have already an acquaintance with it; if not, let me tell you that it is as lovely a bit of land as any that graces the lovely western Riviera of Genoa; full at all seasons of sun, of warmth, of colour, of palm, and lemon, and orange trees. Ariosto had Sanremo in his mind when, describing the voyage of Gano's galley, he brings it in sight of—

> . . . "i monti Ligustici, e Riviera
> Che con aranci e sempre verdi mirti,
> Quasi avendo perpetua primavera,
> Sparge per l'aria i bene olenti spirti."

Sanremo's patent of beauty, you see, does not date from yesterday, nor is it signed by an obscure name. Between you and me, the verses quoted above are not among the most felicitous of the poet, but they are to the point, and therefore I transcribe them. What greater praise can be bestowed upon any spot than to say that it enjoys a perpetual spring? By-the-bye, do not look for my quotation in the pages of the far-famed *Orlando Furioso*, but rather in the first of the less-known *Cinque Canti*, which Ariosto intended as a continuation of his celebrated poem.

Sanremo was the first romance of my boyhood. To it I owe some of the strongest and pleasantest emotions of my young life. My uncle, the canon, had a friend there, to whom he occasionally paid a visit, taking me with him. Now from Taggia to Sanremo it is only an hour-and-a-half's drive; but such was the fuss made about it, and the time of it, and the mode of it—so multifarious were the conditions to which its realization was subjected—that it could not but assume very remarkable proportions in the rather excitable imagination of a boy of eight years old. Indeed, had I had to cross the great Desert, I could not have set out with a keener sense of travelling in right earnest, that delight of all delights at my age, than I did on these occasions, especially the first two or three of them. Habit lessened, but did not wear out the impression.

Each of the trips formed quite an epoch in my life. I dreamed of nothing else for a whole fortnight previous—and oh! how my heart would leap into my mouth at every cloud that rose on the sky, lest it might interfere with our starting; and I dreamed of nothing else for a whole fortnight after. I can still imagine what must have been the peculiar joys of the road—the glory of a seat by the side of Bacciccin, the vetturino—a glory bought at the price of a fib (the fib that I felt sick inside); then the possession of the aforesaid Bacciccin's whip, and the consequent sweet delusion that I was really driving; the patronizing of the respectful peasant boys, who acknowledged my superiority as they passed, and the pulling faces at the disrespectful ones, who refused any such homage—nay, who dared to make fun of me; and last, not least, the trying my skill in making ducks and drakes in the sea during the frequent halts of Bacciccin, who was continually struggling to mend the harness, which was continually breaking, and such like.

As for the joys which I found at Sanremo—our stay there varied from a minimum of two to a maximum of four days—at this distance of time I am sorely puzzled to determine the elements of which they were composed. The palms certainly must have been one of the principal—the palms, the sight of which stirred within me all the poetic feelings of which I was possessed—the palms, on which I doated. As for the rest of the components of my happiness, they were most likely the excitement of novelty, the break in a dreary routine, the exemption from all scholastic tasks, and a *quant. suff.* of liberty of movement. Had the picturesqueness of the landscape, the glorious expanse of the sea, the soft mellowness of the air, anything to do with my enjoyment of Sanremo? I suppose they had, though I might not be conscious of it; the conditions of climate, and the natural beauties of the cosy valley close by—my temporary home—were too little inferior, if so at all, to those of Sanremo, for me to feel the difference; and, as to the sea, of which we had only a distant glimpse from our house, it was too familiar an object to the eyes of one born and brought up in a sea-port town, to produce any overpowering impression on me. I took it for granted, in my innocence, that the whole world was made in the same image as our infinitesimal one. It was only after a long tasting of the piercing fogs of the Thames, and of the bitter blasts of the Seine, that, restored to the land of the myrtle and orange-tree, the boy, now a mature man, could appreciate thoroughly the blessings of these mild Italian skies, and sunny bowers, where winter is only a name, and where, if one was wise, one ought to settle, and refresh both body and mind during at least six months of the year.

Would I might say that I had been that wise man, as I should now be spared the mortification of confessing that my last visit to Sanremo dates as far back as 1857, full seven years ago! The fact is, we do not shape our lives: force of circumstances and habit do it for us, not rarely at the cost of our own inclinations;

thus we arrive at the end of our journey with a sense of bitter wonderment at not having chosen better the stages of it.

Be this as it may, the Sanremo I visited in 1857 had as much improved on that of my boyhood, as the Sanremo of 1864 has improved on that of 1857. Wonderful, is it not, that the little town should have found seven years suffice for a stride forwards, to accomplish the like of which had previously cost her a period equal to that of the wandering of the Jews after their escape from bondage! Surely, to account for this result, there must have been something else at work besides the law of progress, some strong impellent motive. And it was so.

Have you never seen a beauty, strong in her native charms, disdain the aid of all ornaments so long as her heart is yet silent? Well, see that same beauty the moment her heart has spoken, and you will find her abounding in devices for pleasing. This was the case with Sanremo. Her heart, yet mute in 1857, suddenly began to speak in the following year, or thereabouts, and she grew coquettish at once. Yes, Sanremo fell in love with . . . . But I am betraying a secret before the proper time.

Let us return instead to the Sanremo of 1857. The change which struck me most was its new approach. Formerly you entered it by a narrow, irregular road;

now it was by what the French would call a broad *boulevart*, running parallel to the sea, through the whole length of the town. The fashionables of the locality had chosen it, as well they might, for their favourite walk. But even the word *boulevart* does not give a just idea of its charms. Who knows of another *boulevart* flanked on both sides by such gardens as flourish there!—smiled upon by such a sky and sea as shine and sparkle there!—and which wears in its cap two such fine feathers as the two secular palm-trees waving yonder! Therefore allow me to say that the entrance, or *boulevart*, of Sanremo is indeed worth looking at.

The other welcome novelty which gladdened my eyes was a handsome new street, which, starting at right angles from the Boulevart of the Palms, goes straight towards the sea. The Sanremaschi have called it Via Gioberti—one of those excellent ideas which carry along with them their reward, for by doing honour to the memory of a great Italian they have done honour to themselves. I noticed, too, with pleasure, a good sprinkle of freshly-built houses—I was almost tempted to call them palaces, they were so large and handsome. Some were already finished, some only in course of construction. I remarked one, if not two *cafés*, of which I had no recollection; they seemed as clean as they were smart. Most of the shops looked as if they had lately adopted the habit of washing their faces: some few aimed even at elegance. The town had gained an unknown aspect of cleanliness—relative cleanliness, you understand.

But as to hotels it had remained sadly stationary; which, after all, was quite as it ought to be. At the time of which I am speaking, Sanremo was not yet in love—consequently had no desire to please anybody but itself. The improvements which it had realized had had exclusively in view its own comfort and pleasure, and not that of others; now, what could it care about hotels, to which it never went?

So the only hotel of Sanremo continued to be that kept by Signora Angelinin, the hotel "della Palma"— that very same, with the exception of some few microscopic changes for the better, to which in times of yore I had more than once accompanied my uncle, the canon, not to take up our quarters there, but to pay a visit to the landlady. The most that could be said in behalf of the hotel "della Palma" was, that it was decent. One certainly would not have chosen it as a place of abode for any length of time; but the traveller detained by business or stress of weather might easily have passed a week or so there, without being too much to be pitied. The cooking department of "La Palma" enjoyed a well-deserved renown, and Signora Angelinin had the reputation of being very civil and attentive. As for the house itself, nothing could be uglier—outside it was like a barrack, and inside little better than its looks. The distribution of the rooms was inconvenient, and the furniture sparing.

I do not trust for these details to the recollections of my boyhood, but rather to impressions received at a far later date. Between 1847 and the present day I have had frequent opportunities of enjoying the good cheer of the "Palma," though I rarely passed the night there. The hostess had by that time gone to her long rest, and her son and heir reigned over the hotel in her stead. Signor Angelino, some fifteen years ago, was a very handsome young fellow, the very picture of careless content, withal extremely good-natured. He had a passion for fowling, to gratify which he brought up in cages all sorts of small birds, especially blackbirds and nightingales, a task which does not lack its difficulties. Nightingales are queer things to deal with; they rarely survive the loss of their liberty. Busy with his birds, Signor Angelino of course did not work himself to death for the benefit of his customers. Why should he? He had no competition to fear; the hotel was well frequented; the diligences from Nice and from Genoa stopped there daily for dinner; most of the vetturini did the same, and the young landlord's purse filled apace.

For me personally Signor Angelino was always overflowing with attention; and I must do him the justice to say that I invariably found at his house, besides an excellent dinner, an additional dish of *buona cera*, to use a picturesque Italian expression. With one exception, though; and this was on the occasion of my last visit to Sanremo in 1857. The fare was, as usual, excellent, but mine host's reception left something to be desired. Polite as it was, I was sensible that there was an absence of that hearty cordiality to which he had accustomed me. For instance, instead of bestowing on me the light of his countenance, as had been his habit, during the meal, he held entirely aloof. Even the dirty little fellow who waited on me, whistling all the while, showed me a clouded visage. It was not his whistling almost into my ear—not an unprecedented process—that gave me umbrage; it was his uncommunicativeness, so contrary to his nature, which struck me as premeditated. However, when I had paid my bill and left the hotel, I forgot these trifling incidents.

On my way to the convent of the Capuchins I stepped into a shop, where I was well known, to buy a cigar. The man behind the counter handed me the cigars in silence, as he would have done to a stranger. I thought he had not recollected me, and I told him so. He said that he remembered me perfectly. I asked about his wife and children. The answer was laconic: "They are well, I thank you." Surely the man was labouring under the same difficulty of speech that afflicted Signor Angelino and the little waiter of "La Palma." A strange coincidence, thought I; perhaps one of those epidemics, like typhus or miliary fever, which suddenly lay hold of a whole town, or even district. A benign malady, after all, this, which I was beginning to detect, for is it not written that in the "multitude of words there wanteth no sin"? We'll see, at all events, if Padre Tommaso has caught the infection.

I was ringing the bell of the convent door as I thus reflected. Padre Tommaso is a worthy Capuchin friar, and an old friend of mine. I made his acquaintance many, many years ago at Taggia; and, since he has been stationed at Sanremo, I never fail, whenever I go thither, to call on him. Well, was it a delusion on my part, or had Padre Tommaso really caught the infection? He said he was glad to see me, but he did not look as if he were so. He inquired if I intended to stay any time at Sanremo, and my reply in the negative seemed to relieve him. On former occasions he had always pressed me to stay. There were in his countenance and manner unmistakable signs of embarrassment. He found little to say, though it was evident he was doing his utmost to be talkative; the conversation flagged so pitiably that after a few minutes of mutual discomfort I rose to go.

"By-the-bye," he said, rising also, speaking in a tone too careless not to be assumed; "by-the-bye, you have written a book; at least so I have been told."

"Quite true," I replied. "You have not read it, I see."

"Not I," said the padre; "but I have heard it spoken of by those who have. It appears that you make mention of this place."

"True again. I have described it, and many of the beautiful localities of the neighbourhood."

"I hope," continued the padre with more emotion than the occasion seemed to me to warrant, "that you have not treated Sanremo too harshly."

"Treat Sanremo harshly!" cried I astonished; then I added, half laughing, "Had I tried to do so I should have been in the predicament of Balaam, forced to bless in spite of himself."

Padre Tommaso did not look convinced by what I stated, and I frankly told him so.

A slight flush suffused the reverendo's features as he made answer that what I said he was bound to believe; he could not doubt my word; and upon this we separated.

That same evening, as we were taking a cup of tea together in my little den at Taggia, I communicated to my friend and doctor Signor Martini my impressions of the day at Sanremo, among which naturally figured those produced on me by the coldness of mine host of the "Palma" and the tobacconist, and especially by the alteration which I thought I had remarked in Padre Tommaso's manner to me.

Doctor Martini smiled his quiet smile, and said, "Since it has come to this, I may as well tell you all about it. Perhaps I have been stupid to conceal it from you; but the fact is that Sanremo has taken umbrage at a certain passage in 'Doctor Antonio,' which in their eyes is highly disparaging to their town and its environs."

(I ought to have said before that an Italian translation of "Doctor Antonio" had appeared towards the end of 1856.)

"A passage disparaging to Sanremo, or any inch of the Riviera!" cried I in amazement. "If you can show me a word anything but laudatory as to all this part of the country, I will go barefoot, a rope round my neck, and perform public penance to Sanremo."

"Give me a copy of 'Doctor Antonio,'" said the doctor, "and I will point out to you the paragraph incriminated. Here it is, at page five, first chapter:—
"'What is the name of this place?' asks Miss Davenne. 'Sanremo,' is the answer. Sir John Davenne does not approve of the name, at least one may argue as much from his pursed-up lips as he hears it. He looks up the street, and down the street, and finally draws in his head. Had Sir John Davenne kept a note-book, he would probably have made an entry of this sort: 'Sanremo, a queer-looking place; narrow, ill-paved streets; high, irregular houses; ragged people; swarms of beggars;' and so on for a

"whole page. Fortunately for the public reputation
"of Sanremo, Sir John kept no note-book."

"But, my dear friend," said I, "it is as clear as
the sun at noonday that the sentiment here expressed
is not the author's; it is put in the mouth of a fasti-
dious Englishman, who loathes every thing and every
place that is not English. The very exaggeration of
the expression 'swarms of beggars,' while there are in
reality only two, not to speak of the context and the
spirit of the whole sentence, points clearly to its pre-
judiced source."

"Just so," said the doctor; "and the trying to
render which comprehensible to your critics has nearly
given me a pneumonia; but I might as well have
saved myself the trouble and risk. Passion is blind,
you know; and there remains the passage with its
ugly words."

"But there are other passages in the book," said I,
taking it up, "which ought to have rectified any false
impressions created by the one in question; this, for
instance, at page 163, eleventh chapter:—'Sir John
'had ridden over to Sanremo to inspect a garden re-
'commended to his notice by Dr. Antonio. The owner
'of the garden had himself shown Sir John over the
'grounds, and placed all the plants at the baronet's
'disposal. "A most gentlemanlike person," Sir John
'asserted. What a pity (says the author), what a pity,
'Sir John, you do not keep a note-book now!' Is not

this tantamount to saying in so many words, 'Your first hasty judgment on Sanremo was the offspring of ignorance and prejudice; better taught by experience, you would do it more justice now?'"

The doctor, after musing a little, proposed that I should put in writing what I had just said, and send it to one of the Genoese newspapers popular at Sanremo, adding, "It would be an infinite satisfaction to the town."

I answered that I would think the matter over, and so I did; but before I had made up my mind I was called away from Italy. Other scenes, other occupations, other cares engrossed my attention; and, as time slipped on, so all about this *quid pro quo* slipped also out of my recollection, to loom on me again only the other day, when, as I have said at the beginning of this paper, happening to be again in the vicinity of Sanremo, my heart prompted me to go and pay it a visit.

PART II.

THERE being only five vehicles for hire at Taggia, to make sure of one, I sent word to Bernardino, the evening previous to my intended trip, to let me know if I could have his carriage for the next day. Bernardino is one of the five Automedons of Taggia. An answer in the affirmative had scarcely arrived when

Doctor Martini entered, and exclaimed hurriedly, "I have this minute come from Sanremo, and I am commissioned to entreat you not to go thither to-morrow." The Doctor was heated, and, as it seemed to me, in a state of exasperation; seeing which, I jumped to the hasty conclusion that his errand might have some sort of connexion with that absurd story of seven years ago. I said accordingly, half laughing, half provoked, "Why shouldn't I go! Does Sanremo still thirst after my blood? Am I to be hanged or only pelted? Which is it to be?"

"Indeed, I would not guarantee your not being killed with—kindness," said the Doctor, whose elation I had mistaken for exasperation. Doctor Martini has a weakness—that of seeing me not such as I am, but such as the magnifying-glass of his friendship represents me to be; and, whenever he sees what he calls justice done me, he sparkles like a glass of champagne. "Fancy," continued he, "they have planned to send their band to meet you!"

"Mercy on me!" cried I; "you were indeed quite right to advise me not to go."

"Not on account of the band—for, knowing your horror of anything like fuss, I battled hard against the band, and carried my point. They have another reason for wishing you to delay your visit. You must know that, as soon as it transpired that you were at Taggia —and the fact was only public yesterday morning—

the Town Council met, and named a deputation of three members, the mayor and two councilmen, to wait upon and compliment you. Now, this deputation is to be here to-morrow, and would be plunged in the depths of despair if you were to be beforehand with them."

I was struck dumb—band, deputation, compliments! About what, I should like to know. All that I claimed from Sanremo was that it should be just, and behold! it chose to be generous to the verge of extravagance! There was nothing for it, however, but to take the wind as it blew, and send to Bernardino counter-order for the morrow, and a fresh order for the day after that.

Next day, in fact, about two in the afternoon, a carriage stopped at the door, and three gentlemen alighted—the deputation, of course. I gave orders that they should be instantly introduced, and, taking for granted that the most portly of the three was the mayor—queer that he should have such an English face though?—I went up to him with outstretched hand, and said, "Signor Sindaco. . . ."

"I am no Sindaco," said the gentleman addressed, in the raciest English, "I am Doctor Whitley, an English resident at Sanremo, who . . ."

"Very glad to make your acquaintance; pray be seated," said I, and turning to his next neighbour, I reiterated, "Signor Sindaco."

"I am no Sindaco, but Mr. Congreve, also an English resident at Sanremo."

"Very glad to see you;" and, pointing to a chair, I turned to the remaining visitor, my last resource, and began once again, "Signor Sindaco," to which the answer this time came in good Italian, "Non sono il Sindaco, sono il Dottor Panizzi."

"Welcome," said I aloud, and thought *in petto*, "Where can this Sindaco be? What has become of the deputation?"

My fellow-countryman apparently read my perplexity in my face, for he hastened to explain how he and his two companions came to be where they were. But first I must tell the reader that Signor Panizzi is a physician in good practice at Sanremo, who does not give himself out to be the real and genuine Doctor Antonio, as I am told some others do, but rests satisfied with being himself—the modest, well-informed, and gentlemanly person that he is. And let me take this opportunity to declare that Doctor Antonio, good, bad, or indifferent as he may be, is an original picture of my own, and nowise a copy, and that consequently nobody sat for it, or could sit for it.

To return to Doctor Panizzi. He explained to me how, at the very moment of starting for Taggia, the mayor had received a telegram from Turin, which necessitated his immediately convoking the Town Council. The telegram concerned the payment in advance of the land-tax for 1865—a measure which, be it said *en passant*, created that noble race among the municipal bodies of the Peninsula, as to which should be foremost to pay. The mayor had politely expressed the wish that I should be informed of the delay and its cause, as well as of the intention of the deputation to present themselves without fail on the morrow; and Doctor Panizzi had kindly volunteered to bring me the message, upon which the two English gentlemen had proposed to accompany him.

I thanked the ambassador, as I best could, for his kindness, and also his companions, for the honour they had conferred on me by their visit, and then we had a little desultory chat on sundry subjects; and if, on after-thought, my visitors were only half as pleased with me as I was with them, I may thank my lucky stars indeed.

Bernardino, for the second time, received a counter-order for the following day, and a fresh order for the one after, with something else to boot to allay his just impatience.

The deputation kept its appointment this time; true to its word, it arrived next morning. The identification of the mayor proved the source of a fresh blunder on my part. The gentleman whom from his expansiveness I singled out as the chief magistrate turned out to be only a common councilman. He had been a great friend of my uncle the canon, and had known me as a boy, which accounted for the warmth of his greeting. The other councilman had been a schoolfellow of mine at Genoa. I was really touched and grateful for the pleasure they manifested at meeting me again after the lapse of so many years. The only stranger was the mayor, but in a twinkling we were excellent friends.

Many flattering things were said to me, which I need not repeat—among others, that Sanremo owed me a good deal already, and that it hoped to owe me still more. The good I had done Sanremo, they explained, was the sprinkle of English residents that I had sent thither—the good which they expected was the far greater number of British gentry whom they hoped I would send.

I answered, after returning thanks for such a flattering opinion of my influence in England, that I was sorry to see that the Sanremaschi were labouring under a delusion, which I must needs destroy; for, as I was in no way disposed to accept the responsibility of the future, so I must decline all credit for the past. The honest truth then was, that I had not had it in my power, nor, in all likelihood ever would have it in my power to send any one to Sanremo ("No, no," and other strong protests against this declaration). I insisted that I was stating a fact. I had perhaps contributed to some extent in attracting the attention of some foreign tourists towards the Riviera; that might be true (emphatic assent), but I was bound to say that, not for a whole cargo of Doctor Antonios would a single Englishman have stayed there for a week, had he not found a *quant. suff.* of the desiderata no Englishman ever dispenses with—salubrity, cleanliness, and comfort. Let Sanremo increase the amount of comfort which it can offer to its visitors, and a good harvest of them would not fail to Sanremo!

The deputation said *una voce* that my advice should be followed, but that I must promise to stand by them, and held to it more than ever that "I could an if I would" render them marvellous service. This *parti pris* of theirs to make me the pivot of their hopes astounded, nay alarmed, me the more that it was entertained not by ordinary people, but by gentlemen of education and learning, who ought to have known better. I know by sad experience that the Tarpeian rock lies close by the Capitol.

In the meantime my faithful steward and friend, Berenger, had by the luckiest chance disinterred from some nook a bottle of champagne—*rara avis* in those parts—and I challenged my guests to drink to the prosperity of Sanremo, which was done with enthusiasm. I next proposed the toast of the Town Council of Sanremo—that enlightened and deserving body, to whose intelligence, perseverance, and fine taste it was owing, that the charming town they represented had become such an eligible abode for the rich, the invalid, the searchers after novelty of all countries. Encouraged by the applause with which this preamble was received, I went on to say, not without a purpose, "Of course I speak from hearsay, for as yet I have had no opportunity of visiting Sanremo, and forming an estimate of what has been accomplished in improvements and embellishment; but from what I have been told, I do not hesitate even now to declare, and to declare emphatically, that the future of Sanremo is in the hands of Sanremo itself. . . ."

"No, no — *in yours*," shouted three voices in chorus.

"Gentlemen," I replied, "believe me when I say that it is given to no single individual to work out such collective results as you count upon from me . . ."

"But you can if you will," repeated the three voices.

I mused a little; then said, "I regret to observe that you still persist in greatly over-rating my influence, or abilities. It is my desire and intention that there should be no misapprehension between us. The little that I can do, I willingly promise to do, and it is this: I will go to Sanremo, keep my eyes wide open, and afterwards write down my impressions of all I have seen there, and then do my best to have them published."

This assurance put an end apparently to all divergence of opinion between the deputation and me—I say apparently, for at the bottom their estimate and my estimate as to the results likely to arise from the realization of my promise, were as wide apart as they could well be. However, they protested that it was just what they wished — they could desire nothing better; and we parted as cheerfully as we had met; no small boast, considering the errand on which they came.

This time, thank God, I had not to countermand the order for the carriage on the morrow. But man proposes and God disposes. The counter-order came from a quarter which there is no withstanding; the whole of the following morning it did not rain but pour, and, the period of my staying at Taggia drawing towards an end, I began to entertain serious apprehensions lest I should have to put off my survey of Sanremo to next year, or indeed the next after that. Who could tell?

Yes, gentle reader, it rains at Taggia, and even at Sanremo. But be not alarmed; it rains very seldom —too seldom, I was going to say. In the last-named locality there are from 40 to 50 wet days in the year, divided thus: 15 to 20 in the autumn, 12 to 15 in the winter, 10 to 15 in the spring, and 5 to 6 in the summer. Altogether you may count on 250 fine days —really fine sunny days. One might be satisfied with less; what do you say?

Fortunately the weather got out of its fit of sulks quickly, as it generally does in these latitudes. The sky cleared towards the evening, and on the morrow there was not a cloud to intercept the brightness of the sun's rays. By ten o'clock in the forenoon, now in the warm sunshine, oftener under the light mysterious shade of the overhanging olive-trees, we had cleared at a brisk trot the short inland cut which separates Taggia from the high road to Nice, and, turning to the right, were traversing the small hamlet of Arma, the head-quarters at present of the engineers and workmen employed on the railroad, which, in a couple of years, is to bind in its iron grasp the whole of the Riviera from Genoa to Nice. Here is a change indeed from the days of my boyhood!—a change whose result will be nothing less in due time than a radical transformation for the better in the intellectual and economical conditions of the country.

At this point the wide sea bursts upon view, and one's spirits expand with the spreading horizon, and dance with the waves breaking softly on the beach, along which the road continues to wind. But what huge rock is that yonder rising from out the sea? I do not recollect having ever remarked it before. "That is Corsica," replied Bernardino, laughing in his sleeve. Bless me, so it was! I had seen it hundreds of times formerly from Genoa, looming in the distance, but never once in my life standing in such distinct relief against the sky. Some optical phenomenon made it appear so close that really one might have thought of hiring a boat in the belief that it could be reached in a couple of hours. It was a sight worth seeing.

In less than an hour after we were passing by the numerous country-houses which, scattered among vines and orange groves, form a smiling suburb to Sanremo, on this its eastern side. Here I stood up.... I have forgotten to say in its proper place, and I repair the omission, that I had left the inside of the carriage to my companions, who must excuse me if, for brevity's sake, I keep them out of sight, and that, to enjoy the prospect more fully, I had perched myself on the box by the side of Bernardino. So then I stood up, and, peering earnestly before and behind, to the right and the left, and up and down the road, and descrying not the least trace of the dreaded city band, I made bold to desire Bernardino to drive at a slow pace through the town, and not to stop for any call, or halt whatever, until we reached the Convent of the Cappucini, which lies quite at the western extremity of Sanremo.

I had a double motive for acting thus. First of all, I wished to pay my respects to my old friend Padre Tommaso, and I apprehended that, if I delayed my call until I had met Doctor Panizzi, whose guests we were to be, other calls and sight-seeing might interfere with my visit to the Capuchin. Padre Tommaso had last seen me under a threatening cloud, and I was not sorry to show myself to him now, basking in the sunshine of popularity, and taking "fortune's buffets and rewards with equal thanks."

My second motive was that the impressions I might receive from what I was about to see, should be quite spontaneous and perfectly uninfluenced by those of others.

The order to Bernardino had not been given a minute before we came upon a building which I was sure was new. It was a beautiful mansion to our left, with a neat sweep up to the door, and shut off from the road by high iron rails. It bore inscribed on its front, "Hôtel Victoria." Prepared as I was for something very handsome in the way of hotels, I confess that the reality surpassed my expectations; and I had not quite recovered from my agreeable surprise, when lo, and behold! another new house confronts me, this time on my right. This also has a nice sweep, and this also is an hotel, as an inscription in cubital letters —"Hôtel d'Angleterre"—informs wayfarers. Another two minutes, and we enter Sanremo by the beautiful boulevart that you know. My eyes naturally search for the long and well-known Hotel della Palma, and instead of its grim familiar face find the . . . "Hôtel de la Grande Bretagne." Where is the old barrack gone? With the new name, it seems, it has put on a new skin, and a very pleasing one. Upon my word, thought I, a much larger place than this might well be proud of three such hotels. I must have thought aloud, for Bernardino said, "There is a fourth, sir." "A fourth! let us go and look at it;" and at five minutes' distance, past a turning of the road, there towered above us what we might have taken for a palace, but for the name inscribed on its façade, "Hôtel de Londres."

So we say Hôtel de Londres, Hôtel de la Grande Bretagne, Hôtel Victoria, Hôtel d'Angleterre — four titles which are tantamount to a formal declaration. The reader has not waited till now to guess Sanremo's secret. Yes, Sanremo is in love with the English — Sanremo has been in love with the English for many years past. There's nothing that Sanremo will not do to propitiate the English. Sanremo will build more hotels, will lay out more new streets, will commit any extravagance. Sanremo is ready, in order to make room for its wished-for guests, to do like the Romans of old, go and bivouac on any of the seven hills on which it is said to stand. But Sanremo must have plenty of English, or die.

On our way back to the Convent we met Doctor Panizzi in hot chase of us; so we got out of the carriage, and, after a cordial greeting given and received, it was agreed that my companions should go shopping (Sanremo is a little capital for Taggia and the surrounding small towns), and that the Doctor should accompany me to Padre Tommaso. We rang, and rang, and rang the Convent bell for a quarter of an hour at least without succeeding in bringing anybody to the door. It was the hour, I suppose, of the monks' meditation; so, our time being short, I gave up in despair Padre Tommaso, and went instead, as it was my duty to do, to pay my respects to the Mayor and the gentlemen of the deputation. This done, we joined our shopping friends on the boulevart, as we had previously settled, and walked *viribus unitis* to our head-quarters to be, the Hôtel d'Angleterre.

Had I had any option in the matter, which was not the case, and, as it seems, could not be the case, it would have been the hotel of my choice for the simple reason that the landlord was my old acquaintance, Signor Angelino of the "Palma." But Doctor Panizzi, when he had done me the honour of coming to see me at Taggia, had explained to me that I could not go to any one of the Sanremo hotels upon my own account without the certainty of offending, if not injuring, the other three,—an inconvenience that might be remedied, however, if I, with my party of course, would consent to be his guests at an hotel of his own choosing. I confess I did not much see the difference; still, considering the earnestness with which the proposal was urged, I thought it wise to comply with it. Perhaps it was only a blind to induce me to accept of the Doctor's hospitality.

Be this as it may, here we were at the Hôtel d'Angleterre, shaking hands with Signor Angelino, who was waiting for us at the door, and whose reception of me did not lack in cordiality this time. Dinner would be on the table within ten minutes—a not unwelcome announcement—and perhaps in the meantime, suggested the landlord, it might amuse us to take a look at the internal arrangements of the Hotel. We asked for nothing better. We accordingly went over the whole house: it is not large, and it was therefore easy to inspect all the details; and the more we saw the greater our surprise and gratification. It was like a dream to me, who could contrast the past with the present, to find myself in a Sanremo hotel replete with every comfort which characterizes a good Swiss inn, that perfection of its kind. Carpets everywhere, stairs included, well-furnished sitting-rooms, nice white-curtained bedrooms, good iron bedsteads, mirrors and dressing-tables, washhand-stands with every appliance for ablutions, all other proper arrangements, fireplaces in every room, and abundance of arm-chairs and sofas. Some of the windows open into balconies, and all command a fine view, over intervening sloping wooded banks, of the sea, and of the town, climbing pyramid-like up its verdant hills; not to mention the sight of the road below, which, being a thoroughfare, and, besides, a favourite lounge of the residents, is not wanting in animation and attraction, especially at certain hours. The Hôtel d'Angleterre seems built on purpose for persons of a sociable, yet shy temperament, who, though appreciating the advantages of an isolated position, and of the free play of the air, and the absence of bad smells which it secures, yet enjoy feeling themselves in some sort of communication with their fellow-creatures. Sketchers especially, and lovers of picturesque groups, will find here ample and not-to-be-despised pabulum for their brush or pencil.

Nothing could be more cheerful than the *salle à manger*, where we sat down to dinner, with its fine prospect and gaily-painted ceiling—nothing more inviting than the dinner-table, with its rich display of snow-white damask, silver, and glass, all glancing in the reflex of a bright Italian November sun. Signor Angelino, dressed in a smart black coat, took his place at the hospitable board, and did the honours in excellent style, and in a most cordial spirit. We were waited upon no longer by the dirty whistling little fellow, but by a couple of good-sized, clean-looking, black-coated, regular waiters.

The dinner was capital, and so were the wines. At dessert we had a plentiful supply of champagne, and hearty were the toasts we drank to the prosperity of the Hôtel d'Angleterre. Might all the expense and care lavished on it be repaid four-fold; might it soon be chokeful with guests from cellar to attic!

"May God hear you!" said Signor Angelino, with emotion; "for, if the English don't come, I don't know how it will fare with me; or rather, I know too well. I have staked upon this undertaking my all, and their all," pointing to his wife and daughters, who just then entered.

As he spoke, I for the first time remarked a certain alteration in his appearance. He had still the open blue eye of yore, and the frank, good-humoured face, but its once careless expression had fled from it. It was the same landscape, only there was no longer any sun on it.

"God will help us, and so will Signor Giovanni," said Signora Angelino, with an appealing glance to me. (It is customary in those parts to address people by their Christian names.)

"My dear signora," I replied, "I have only good wishes to give, and those are sincerely yours."

"Ah, Signor Giovanni, you can give something better than wishes, if you have the will," urged Signor Angelino. "You know the English; you can bring them to us; you brought the first who ever came here, you know."

It was as touching as it was absurd to see these simple-minded people pinning their success upon a retired student, as though he was a lord of the land, or a potent star of fashion. It was of no use to argue the point; so I contented myself with a still stronger declaration of my utter want of power, and at the same time of my good will.

"We were just on the move to go and visit the other hotels, as I had been invited to do through Doctor Panizzi, when a messenger brought me a very nicely engraved plan of Sanremo, sent by the Marquis Borea, together with a request that I would do him the favour to come and pay him a visit. Straitened for time as I was, I could not refuse an old schoolfellow—one, moreover, nearly connected with a much-valued cousin of mine; so I went first to the marquis. Besides the natural and sincere wish to shake hands with an old friend, I found that the marquis had a second object in view in inviting me to his palazzo, for palazzo it is. He was desirous of showing me a part of it, which he had at last been persuaded to think of letting. Only the year before he had declined to let it to a very distinguished English lady, the Lady Herbert. But since then the current had become too strong even for him to resist, and he now also put in his claim for my patronage. My former schoolfellow, to my sorrow, shared in the general infatuation as to my powers of attraction.

"I went over the apartment in question, a description of which, if at all adequate to its merits, would take more space than I can dispose of. I will only say that it is a princely suite of rooms, and that everything about it, size, pictures, furniture, &c. has that impress of grandeur which is a distinctive trait of a real Italian palace. It has an interest of another kind; it was there that Napoleon I. and Pope Pius VII. each passed a night. You can see the bedchamber unaltered in any respect since those personages occupied it. Annexed to the apartment is an enormous terrace, which brings to mind the Hanging Garden of Babylon.

As I came out of the Borea Palace, I was met by a priest, who wished me to go and inspect Villa Gnecco, a country house not more than ten minutes' walk from the town, and I was apologizing for my inability to do so, when a gentleman accosted me, and said he hoped I would honour with my presence the Casino, or Reading-room; and following close on the heels of this gentleman came another, with a third application on behalf of the School, or Liceo as they call it, of the town. I felt somewhat in the predicament of *Figaro* in the "Barbière"—

> "Figaro qua, Figaro là;
> Uno alla volta, per carità."

In the impossibility of satisfying all demands, I determined in favour of knowledge; that is, I paid a flying visit to the Liceo. The establishment is airy, spacious, and clean, and I have it on good authority that it is well conducted. I can myself bear witness to the kindly manners of the principal, and of the professor of natural philosophy, who received us, as well as to the satisfactory appearance of the rooms appropriated to chemical and physical experiments. Indeed, we had nothing better at the University of Genoa in my time. Parents anxious that their youngsters should not lose their Latin, or forget their rules of three, or whatever they may have learnt as to electricity, may take the hint, and unite *utile dulci*.

On our way back towards the Victoria, my notice was called to a number of eligible houses both in the town and out, and more were mentioned to me, where lodgings could be had. So that persons inclined to prefer the quiet of a private lodging to the life more or less in common of an hotel, will have an *embarras du choix*.

The Hôtel Victoria is a noble edifice indeed, one that would not disgrace a great metropolis. It is on a far larger scale than the Hôtel d'Angleterre, a little further from the town, say five minutes more, and very comfortably and elegantly arranged in every respect. It possesses the advantage of a spacious garden on the side of the house facing the sea, from which the grounds are only separated by a belt of olive-trees. A more quiet, more sunny, or more lovely retreat one cannot imagine for persons in delicate health, who either cannot, or do not care to walk in streets or roads. To such I especially recommend the ground-floor, which opens into the garden. It is delightful. Here also the landlord had a long and anxious face, and of course appealed to me for help—"Mi raccomando a Lei, Signor Dottore." I verily believe that he took me for Doctor Antonio. May Heaven help him and his hotel!

Our next visit was to have been for the Hôtel de la Grande Bretagne; how or why it was that we postponed it till after we had been to the Hôtel de Londres, I cannot say; this I know, that the inspection of the Hôtel de Londres took up so much more time than we had anticipated, and, when at last we had done with it, it was so late, and we were so tired, that we had to give up seeing the Grande Bretagne ourselves. I can therefore only speak of it from report, and report, I am glad to say, speaks highly in its favour.

As we were walking past it on the Boulevart of the Palms, Doctor Panizzi pointed out to me, first, the spot where is to be erected a Protestant chapel—the Municipality have already granted a piece of land for that purpose—and, secondly, the sites of an intended new casino, or reading-room, and of a theatre. There is also a project for opening a new street parallel to Via Gioberti, leading from the boulevart to the sea, and for making a public walk along the edge of the beach—a modest imitation of the "Promenade des Anglais" at Nice—which is certainly one of the most remarkable among the beautiful things of

Europe. But, to realize these plans, a little time and a good deal of money are requisite, and encouragement on the part of those for whose sakes Sanremo chiefly wishes to beautify itself.

To speak only of the present. There already exists at Sanremo a promising germ of an English colony. Last winter it could boast of no less than fifteen families from Great Britain, amounting to nearly one hundred individuals; and let us hope that this present winter will see its numbers doubled. The colony counts among its members an English clergyman—who, until there shall be a chapel, performs divine service in a room—and an English physician, that same Dr. Whitley, who favoured me with his visit at Taggia. Visitors inclined to consult local doctors will find skill, experience, and every care and attention from Doctor Panizzi, of Sanremo, and Doctor Martini, of Taggia—the valued friend and family physician of the writer of these lines. Both are very cautious as to bleeding, and both understand English. I have already said that there is a reading-room or a casino; I must add that there is also a bookseller's shop; both of which might certainly be better provided, the one with newspapers, the other with books; but with them, as with everything else, the supply will increase with the demand. There must be a beginning, you know. There are numerous pleasant walks in the town itself, and in its environs—one especially, that to the Madonna della Costa, which I recommend to all lovers of fine views. They will realize from thence that fine word-picture of Coleridge:—

> ". . . Stand on that sea-cliff's verge
> Where the pine just travail'd by the breeze above
> Makes one soft murmur with the distant surge,
> And *shoot thy* being through earth, sea, and air,
> Possessing all things with intensest love."

But we must not forget that we are bound for the Hôtel de Londres. I visited it from top to bottom, and I cannot speak too highly of all its internal arrangements; they are neatness, comfort, and elegance combined. This Hotel is in a somewhat isolated position, to the west of Sanremo, though only ten minutes from it; but a bend of the road hides Sanremo from view. The prospect is very fine—the eye glides down a gentle verdant declivity till it rests upon the sea—the wide sea spreading to the horizon. To the right a promontory feathered with wood to its utmost edge shuts in a little bay, along whose base lie two dark rocks, against which breaks the silver spray of the waves. The spot would be melancholy, if anything in this bright, smiling atmosphere could look otherwise than cheerful.

The Hôtel de Londres, I will venture to say, will be a favourite resort for persons of a romantic disposition, and especially for poets. It was my good fortune to meet there and be kindly greeted by one. I hope I commit no indiscretion in naming Mr. Sydney Dobell.

Mr. Dobell had some years ago heard of me and my family from a common friend; and, my name coming to his ears as I was paraded through the Hotel, he sent me his card. He was doubly welcome, for his own sake and for that of the absent. We spoke, of course, of Sanremo, and I was very glad to hear him say that, much pleased as he had been with Spain, and the south of France, which he had lately visited, nowhere had he found so sheltered and charming a nook as Sanremo. He inquired affectionately about my mother and brother—both, alas! gone from me—and I was grateful to him for the evident shock of pain which my sad answer gave him. He was silent for a while, and, when he spoke again, it was to quote a passage from Fichte about sons who had made the name of their mothers venerated by every one—a sentiment which went straight to my heart. We parted with a warm shake of the hand, and a good-bye, which conveyed, I am sure, a blessing from both hearts.

The winter sun had set, and it was time to think of a speedy retreat homewards. So our two last visits had to be hurried through—the one to Doctor Panizzi's family, the other to the warm-hearted councilman, the friend of my uncle, the Canon, whom I had missed in the morning. After a cordial farewell, and manifold thanks to Doctor Panizzi for all he had done for us in his double capacity of host and guide, we entered our one-eyed calessino—true it is that the one lamp was big enough for two—and were off. Night by this time had quite closed in—the road was dark, and, owing to the collateral railway works, was here and there rough and rugged, which made prudent Bernardino drive cautiously. The lights of the pretty little town gleaming along the shore and up the hill were the last I saw of it. I waved my hand in token of farewell; then I sank into a vague reverie of its past, present, and future, out of which I was not roused till I arrived at home, and passed from outer darkness to the bright light of my fire and lamp.

And now, gentle reader, if this my chat has succeeded in transfusing into your mind any portion of the charm and poetry with which Sanremo has always been invested in mine, I shall rest satisfied that not in vain have I fulfilled my promise to my friends of Sanremo to bring them before the notice of my English friends.

END OF "SANREMO REVISITED."

A DESIGNING ARISTOCRAT.

A DESIGNING ARISTOCRAT.

Have you ever considered what a grand, what a beautiful thing a tree is? I suspect that trees have not had all the justice done them which they deserve. You often meet people with a hobby for flowers, or for a particular flower, or for mosses or ferns, or what not, but very seldom for trees. And yet what more worthy of admiration than a tree! Take it as a whole, can you conceive a happier combination of majesty and of grace—firm as a rock, yet light as a feather fan? Or take it in its several parts—from the trunk, a masterpiece in itself, if you examine it closely, of texture and colour—from the powerful trunk, I say, able to stand its own against a hurricane, up to the slenderest filigree twig waving in the air, and see without wonder, if you can, the never-ending development, tier upon tier, of gradually dwindling curves, which go to form the glorious arch of its far-spreading canopy. Or look at trees in their relation to the landscape around; why, it derives most of its comeliness, variety, and character from them. Trees are to the face of the earth what those golden or jet black tresses are to yours, fair reader—not all its beauty, certainly, but the indispensable complement to it.

Let us leave this, however, an open question; the fact I have to state is, that Herr von Linden had a passion for trees—by no means an exclusive one, as abundantly shown by the great care he had taken to surround himself with everything that is lovely in nature, as well as trees. Herr von Linden was the master of the Grün (the Green), that model country seat, mentioned with just praise in all the books of travel in Switzerland, and which few tourists, worthy the name, who pass in its vicinity, fail to visit. The Grün, for generations in the von Linden family, was, when inherited by its present owner, in a sad condition of neglect and decay, indeed, with little to recommend it but its unparalleled prospect and fine trees. Herr von Linden had devoted ten years of his life, and a corresponding amount of taste and money (of both which articles he had a large share) to restore, improve, enlarge, and embellish the Grün, in short, to make it what it is now-a-days, one of the attractions and boasts of his country. And at the Grün he spent regularly eight months of every year, in the enjoyment of his flowers, his lawns, his espaliers, his fish-ponds, etc. etc., and, above all, of his favourite trees.

If there be a spot on earth where Herr von Linden's innocent hobby could find full scope for its gratification, it was the district where the Grün was situated. Timber grew there to perfection, and I doubt whether far-famed St. Gingolphe itself could exhibit such glorious specimens of chestnut, walnut, and oak-trees, as graced the park of the Grün and the common outside. Those on the common belonged to the parish, but not the less tenderly for that did Herr von Linden's solicitude extend to them. He paid them regular visits, knew all of them by heart, as it were, and could have drawn an exact picture of the handsomest of them from memory. Unfortunately, this sort of catholic fondness exposed him to frequent disappointments and heartburnings; for the parish entertained no sentimental or æsthetic notions about its trees, but looked upon them with very matter-of-fact eyes, which only saw in them what they would fetch in the market. Those were days of mourning at the castle in which such bargains were concluded; and not a blow of the fatal axe but echoed painfully through the frame of the lord of the castle. So intense, indeed, was his disgust at what he held to be both a profanation and a kind of murder, that for weeks and months after one of these executions, he would not stir out of his own precincts. But Herr von Linden was a stout man of fifty, somewhat plethoric and short-winded, and his doctor, who was also his friend, was for ever prescribing exercise—real exercise, and not mere sauntering, or driving; and thus it would come to pass that, after long demurring, the elderly gentleman, some fine day or other, would put his campstool under his arm, stalk through his park gates along a green lane which skirted the grounds of the Grün for a good mile, and so on till he reached the common, or, according to the alias he had bestowed upon it, "The Field of the Massacre."

There were still not a few remarkable and respectable looking trees, but the superlatively fine had all gone, all but one, either accidentally or intentionally spared—an oak of magnificent dimensions, and of the most perfect beauty. It stood, a glorious beacon, at the junction of the lane with the highway. Herr von Linden would always stop at the distance which secured him the most complete view of this monarch of the common, never failing to say, while opening his campstool, "Let us feast our eyes on that beautiful creature yonder while we can—it won't be for long."

"Suppose you were to buy it," suggested one day his sister, the faithful confidant of his sorrows and companion of his walks.

"Buy it!" repeated von Linden.

"Yes, and so make sure that no one can deprive you of the pleasure of seeing it."

"By Jove! a good idea. I wonder it never came

into my head. Buy it I will, if only the Corporation will sell it."

"The Corporation are too shrewd not to catch at an offer which leaves them their tree, and puts its price in their pocket."

"We shall see," said the brother.

It was market day at the neighbouring little town, and peasant men and women were coming back from it, in couples, in groups, alone; some in carts, most on foot. Herr von Linden hailed a solitary wayfarer, who was passing on his side of the road, and asked him, "Do you belong to the parish of Tattiken?"

The man stopped short, and, staring vacantly at the questioner, took time to consider whether he did or did not belong to it. However, upon the question being again put to him, he replied, yes, that he did live at the village so named.

"And do you know the President?" (another name for the mayor in Switzerland) continued Herr von Linden.

"The President? Karl the Miller? Of course I do!"

"Very well, then; will you have the goodness to tell the President that Herr von Linden wishes to buy that oak yonder—to buy it at the price the Corporation shall think fit to name? and binds himself not to cut it down, or destroy, or damage it in any way, but to preserve it as it is, an ornament to the country. I speak seriously," added Herr von Linden, somewhat sternly, to check a growing disposition in his listener to look would-be knowing; "I speak in downright earnest. I am Herr von Linden, and what I now pledge myself to, I am ready to put on paper and sign. In one word, I propose to buy the oak, pay for it, and leave it as it is—do you understand? You do—very well, I need not detain you any longer. Good afternoon."

Had the message with which he was intrusted been at all an ordinary one ten to one but our man would have forgotten all about it in no time, for honest Peter, let us christen him so, was returning from market, and was therefore in that blessed condition of confirmed tipsiness, in which are the majority of his class returning from market. As it was, the message of which he was the bearer was so novel, and out of the common, that every word of it forced its way into his muddled brain, and floated victoriously there above the fumes of liquor, which kept it spinning like a teetotum. Peter went straight to the inn to do Herr von Linden's message. The inn plays an important part everywhere, but nowhere a more important one than in the canton in which Tattiken is situated; all public and private business is transacted there, *inter pocula;* it is there that the town council hold their sittings, that political or commercial meetings assemble, that litigations are settled, agreements entered into, bargains made, etc. etc. Peter was sure of finding the President there.

The President treated Peter's communication as the ravings of a man in his cups, that is, with supreme incredulity and contempt. Herr von Linden, argued the President, knew better than to pay the price of anything for the mere pleasure of doing so—if any such proposal had really passed his lips, it was merely to amuse himself at the expense of the person he was addressing. Poor Peter was too far gone to make an effectual stand in defence of the authenticity of the proposition, or of the seriousness with which it had been made, and he had to go to his bed utterly snubbed and discomfited.

But when, on the morrow, being sober, or nearly so, he returned to the charge, and insisted and persisted in what he had said, repeating *verbatim* Herr von Linden's own expressions on the subject, the President's incredulity lost somewhat of its pertinacity, and he condescended so far as to admit that the matter ought to be sifted and made clear. To which effect, an hour or so after, both the President and Peter, in their Sunday suits and with Chinese-wall-like shirt collars, were ringing for admittance at the gate of the Grün.

"They bring you the oak," said Jungfrau von Linden, at sight of them.

"Maybe," answered her brother, "but I should wonder much, for they never do aught in a hurry; *chi va piano va sano* is their motto."

He received the visitors in the stone verandah opening on the garden. A servant brought a tray on which were a bottle of wine and two glasses, which he immediately filled. Herr von Linden was known never to drink wine between his meals, and the fact was little to his advantage with his neighbours. The two, being invited so to do, emptied their glasses, which done, the President expounded the object of their visit. Herr von Linden in reply fully confirmed Peter's statement, and answered with perfect good-humour the various questions which the President thought fit to ask. The interview was short, and apparently satisfactory to all parties. The President took leave, promising to seize the earliest opportunity to place before the council Herr von Linden's proposal, and to make known to him the result.

It is recorded of a Parisian that he laid a wager and won it, that he would offer for sale on the Pont Neuf pieces of five francs at half their value, and find no purchasers beyond a certain number, the maximum of whom he fixed at a very low figure. It is rare that too advantageous a bargain does not beget a suspicion of foul play, and the *Timeo Danaos et dona ferentes* is after all a natural feeling. That a man of Herr von Linden's stamp, generous if you will, but of too much good sense to throw money away, should pay for the oak without getting some equivalent, seemed to the President such an absurd notion, that he could not bring himself to entertain it for a moment. And as to ever fancying that this equivalent could be found in the satisfaction of preserving a tree, and the pleasure of looking at it, this was a finesse of sentiment too alien to his nature for him even to dream of it in others. The only conclusion, therefore, at which he could arrive, was that Herr von Linden's proposal concealed a snare, and that the Corporation must look sharp about them if they did not wish to be taken in. The President was too great an authority, and his view chimed in too well with a certain preconception prevalent in the village, not to find favour with most of those to whom it was communicated. Yes, it was clear that there was a snake in the grass, and half the parish went to their beds that night revolving in their minds what could be the hidden insidious purpose which lurked under the apparently fair offer made by Herr von Linden—indeed, looking upon him somewhat in the light of a public enemy.

To account for this feeling, we must say that the eminent personage of whom we are writing, possessed as he was of many of the requisites which make a man popular, yet was far from being so in the parish which owed him so much. The great improvements and embellishments he had effected at the Grün had naturally necessitated an enormous outlay of money; some of which, much or little as it might be, had found its way into each and all of the cottages around; add to which, that the amount of parochial taxes assessed upon him reached a sum far beyond that paid by the whole parish; that no local improvement, or charity, when it passed from theory to practice, but was defrayed by him; that no private misfortune but found alleviation at his hands. Why, then, was he not popular? Simply because he was a *ci-devant*, an aristocrat, which in a canton long ruled by the aristocracy, and only from yesterday in the hands of the purest democracy, meant a man not to be trusted, an adversary, almost an enemy. Did Herr von Linden busy himself with politics, tamper with the electors, use his influence and fortune to secure the return of conservative members? did he in any way oppose, or only by word of mouth traduce the powers that were? Nothing of the sort. Other was the head and front of his offending. That for which Herr von Linden was found fault with, that which made him an aristocrat was, that he had a *Von* prefixed to his name; that his servants wore a livery; that he kept aloof from his neighbours, the peasantry; that while receiving lots of fine ladies and gentlemen at the castle he had never so much as said to any of the best men in the parish, men in authority, men invested by the people with a part of its sovereignty—that to such men he had never so much as said—"Come and have a bottle at the Grün,"—never so much as even shaken hands with them. It was these airs of superiority, as they were styled, which stood between Herr von Linden and popular favour.

To return. We left half the parish occupied in the search after the secret object of Herr von Linden's insidious proposal. There is nothing like seeking in order to find, and by dint of seeking, the President found. Here was his fiat—Herr von Linden aimed at nothing less than the transferring of the oak to his own grounds. There!

Great as was their respect for the President's penetration, and great as was their inclination to find Herr von Linden guilty, the few councilmen extra-officially assembled at the inn, to whom the President imparted his wonderful discovery, received it with unmistakable signs of incredulity. "How could he manage it—an oak of such dimensions—the thing was impossible."

"A moment," cried the President, piqued. "Your incredulity, excuse me for saying so, only proves your ignorance, otherwise you would be aware that lately, in Paris, appliances have been found, by means of which the biggest trees may be uprooted as easily as a bottle is uncorked, and transplanted at any distance.

And who can be sure whether one of these contrivances is not at this very hour in the cellars of the castle, ready for use the moment we sell our oak?"

"But," objected one of the dissidents, "has not Herr von Linden engaged to leave the oak as it is?"

"Ah! to be sure!" was the President's ironical rejoinder, "to leave the oak as it is; but did he engage to leave the oak *where* it is?"

The acuteness of this argument achieved what the information about the Parisian invention had begun—it brought conviction home to all present. Yes, that was it; Herr von Linden wanted to rob them of their tree, to beautify his park at the expense of the parish. It was a shame—a crying shame. Some were for immediately convoking the town council, and rejecting the proposal with public scorn. Others considered that measure insufficient, and contended that the Corporation owed it to themselves to give Herr von Linden a piece of their mind.

"Not before we have heard what he has to say for himself," interposed the President. "Even the greatest culprit has a right to defend himself. Let us proceed legally. Let a deputation wait on Herr von Linden, and hear what he has to say in his own justification."

It was not every day that the Grün could be

entered, and the master thereof brought down to a footing of equality with the Corporation; the occasion was too rare not to be improved. So it happened that the gates of the Grün saw once more the Sunday suit, and the Chinese-wall-like collar of the President, accompanied by two councilmen, pass through them.

At sight of the three approaching, Jungfrau von Linden exclaimed, "This time, brother, you may make sure of your oak."

"This time, I don't say no," answered Herr von Linden; and hastened to receive the deputation. In fact he made so sure of the oak being his own, that he said, in high good humour—"Well, gentlemen, I suppose we may consider the affair as settled."

"Not yet," replied the President; "there is a point or two on which we have to request some elucidations."

Herr von Linden's disappointment and pique at this speech were extreme; he started from his seat as if he had been stung by a wasp, and said, "I have been sufficiently cross-questioned, I peremptorily refuse to give any further explanations. Keep your tree or not, as you please, but leave me my time. I am very busy just now, and must therefore wish you good-day."

So saying, Herr von Linden walked off. The deputation, left alone, looked at each other, looked at the bottle just being brought in by the servant to no purpose, and then took their departure.

The party assembled at the inn had in the meantime received considerable accessions, and expectation was at its highest when the discomfited deputation returned. We renounce the attempt to describe the commotion produced by the account of the reception they had met; it was like the falling of a lighted match upon a heap of dried leaves. What! was this the way the magistrates chosen by the people were to be treated! Treated thus, too, by one who, it might be averred, had been caught with his hand in the pocket of the parish! It was not to be borne. The matter could not be allowed to rest here. An example ought to be made. The Great Council must be instantly memorialized.

A section of the assembly, more heated than the rest (it was composed of those zealous citizens who had sat over their wine for the last three hours), spurned memorializing, and were for doing something —they knew not what, but something awful.

"You will do nothing of the kind, if you will be guided my me," said the President, who chose to act the part of moderator again. "Let us be forbearing to the end. It behoves the representatives of the people to be above all passion. The master of the

Grün—I don't mean to exculpate him, he has been wrong, very wrong, throughout the whole of this affair—but the master of the Grün is entitled to some consideration. Don't let us be hard on him. Don't let us deprive him of the power of explaining and making amends. I move that Herr von Linden be invited to be present at the sitting of the Corporation, which is to be held to-morrow, in order that he may give such explanations as may be deemed necessary."

It needed all the influence and persuasion of the President to carry the motion, not to speak of sundry *apartés*, such as "Don't you see that to have him here is the fullest amends we can desire?" The throw, in fact, was clever enough if it would only catch. To have Herr von Linden there, to have him much in the position of a criminal in the dock, and to sit in judgment upon him, was a double satisfaction, the mere prospect of which was enough to make all mouths water.

The result of the deliberation was, that late in the afternoon of that memorable day, a great *pancarte* was brought to Herr von Linden, which had been left at the lodge by the beadle of the parish. The contents of the document were as follows:—

"Herr von Linden of the Grün is requested by the Corporation of Tattiken to attend the meeting to be held to-morrow at ten A.M., in order that he may give such verbal explanations in reference to his proposal of purchasing the oak as the Corporation may deem advisable to require.

"For the Corporation,
"THE PRESIDENT."

"Upon my word," said Herr von Linden to his sister, "these good people have lost their wits," and he forthwith wrote a few hasty lines upon the outside of the envelope he had just received, and sent it back at once to the President. The lines were as follows:—

"In answer to the enclosed communication, the undersigned begs to inform the Corporation of Tattiken that he withdraws purely and simply his application to become the purchaser of the oak.

"H. VON LINDEN."

In the afternoon of the next day, another big envelope was deposited at the castle, the contents of which ran thus: —

"The undersigned is commissioned by the Corporation of Tattiken to lay before Herr von Linden the decision as to his application.

"And first of all disposing of the incident raised by Herr von Linden's communication of yesterday:

"The Corporation in council assembled has unanimously declared the withdrawal of Herr von Linden's proposal to be illegal, void, and of no effect.

"Passing to the merit of the application itself:

"Considering the insufficiency and unsatisfactoriness of the explanations vouchsafed by Herr von Linden,

"Considering his refusal further to enlighten either the deputation sent to him for that purpose, or the whole Corporation according to invitation,

"The Corporation in council assembled in date of this day, have, with one voice resolved,

"That it would be inconsistent with their dignity, and unsafe for the interests of the parish, to take into consideration Herr von Linden's said application.

"For the Corporation,
"THE PRESIDENT."

Herr von Linden was so shocked by this piece of impertinence, altogether so embittered by the gratuitous ill-will evinced towards him throughout all this business, that he left the Grün with his sister, and went to travel.

Shortly after his departure, the tree, the innocent cause of all this ill blood, was sold to a railway contractor, and disappeared. If you pass through Tattiken, the villagers will point out to you the place where it once stood, and tell you to this day of the narrow escape the parish had of being cheated of their oak by a designing aristocrat of the neighbourhood.

END OF "A DESIGNING ARISTOCRAT."

A DEED OF DARKNESS.

A DEED OF DARKNESS.

WHEN, after a forced absence (from political motives) of fifteen years, I was enabled in 1848 to go back to my own country, one of the first persons to welcome my return was an old fellow student, whose name had not so much as once met my eye or my ear for the last twelve years, and whose existence I had wellnigh forgotten.

Curzio and I were of about the same age, had been at school and college at the same time in Genoa, had, without being very intimate, sown some of our wild oats together, and were actually embarked in the same political boat when it capsized. How he managed to keep afloat while I sunk, and by what concourse of circumstances we came to lose sight of each other for so long, are matters irrelevant to my purpose. Suffice it to say that Curzio called on the morrow of my arrival, and looked so pleased to see me, spoke of old times so feelingly, and of myself so affectionately, that his genial warmth told upon me instantly, and I came up to his temperature in no time. In looks he was scarcely altered, but his manner and conversation were singularly improved. He talked well and a good deal, for which he humorously apologized by saying that he had been gagged all his life and that he must now make up for lost opportunities. Meeting after so long a separation in such eventful times, we ran no risk of lacking topics of conversation. We spent a few hours together very agreeably, at the end of which we both made the pleasant discovery that we had never been such good friends as we were now.

"You must come and see me in my wilds," said he, as he was leaving.

"Of course I shall, as soon as I have a little leisure," said I.

"I cannot take a put off," he replied; "ripe grapes cannot wait; you must really contrive to come within the week. I have something like a vintage to tempt you, a rarity not to be disdained now-a-days."

That it was a rarity I knew to my cost, for this was the second year that, owing to the oidium, my vineyards had not yielded a single grape. In short, he insisted with so much good grace on my naming a day, that I named it.

The little town of the Riviera of Genoa, in which Curzio lived, was three hours' walk from that in which I had pitched my tent for the time being. It stood half way up a hill crowned by ilex and olive, and—

shall I be permitted to add, that it commanded a beautiful view of land and sea? I know that descriptions of natural scenery are *rococo* in our sensational days, and I would fain not be behind my time. I was received with the utmost cordiality by the master and the mistress of the house. The lady was a brunette, full of character, and I made speedily great friends with a bevy of black-eyed, curly-headed little fellows, who had none of the squeamish bashfulness of their age. My host had convoked for the occasion the *ban* and *arrière ban* of the notabilities of the neighbourhood, and there was a pretty large number present. Let me not forget to say that my old school-fellow was mayor of the town, doctor of the parish, and the largest landowner therein: three qualifications which combined to make him socially, as he was intellectually, the first personage of the place.

The vineyard whose golden riches were destined to fall under our knives and scissors, was scarcely half an hour distant from Curzio's house in the town. It was nearly noon when we proceeded to it *en masse*, and began our harvest. It is merry work and a pretty sight this gathering of grapes, especially when enlivened, as it was in the present case, by the never-ceasing prattle and gladdening turbulence of a dozen joyous small busybodies taking their share, and more than their share, in it. There is something intoxicating in the process. It seems as though the gentle stimulant virtually contained in the juicy fruit asserted its exhilarating powers beforehand.

My host told me the lucky chance to which was owing the relative preservation of this vineyard from the prevalent disease. The first year he had been as great a sufferer as his neighbours; only one vine, which grew against his house, had, by a strange exception, brought forth healthy fruit. What might be the cause of this phenomenon? By dint of seeking, it recurred to his memory that one day, from the window of his laboratory, below which grew the vine, he had let fall by chance a bag full of sulphur, which spread itself over the whole plant. Acting upon this datum, he had tried sulphur next year on his vineyard amid the sneers of all round, and the present fine vintage was the result.

"They ought to raise a statue to you," said I.

"I should be well contented if they would only profit by my experience," answered my friend, "but they won't; I am sure they won't for twenty years to come. They are the slaves of routine and habit; everything in the shape of novelty, however beneficial, including the statutes and self-government, is a dead letter to them."

After expatiating at some length and with some warmth on this theme, he suddenly paused, then added, with some compunction, "I would not prejudice you too much against these good folks, for good they are, and have many excellent points. A more docile, sober, much-enduring population can hardly be met with; there is a natural mildness in their blood, which renders deeds of violence impossible to them. Crime, one may say, is unknown in these parts; only do not speak to them of progress, they are impervious to it."

He spoke well and willingly, as I have already remarked, and as I derived both pleasure and instruction from what he said, I managed to remain by his side during all the process of the vintage. A thorough practical man, familiar with the best methods of local cultivation, perfectly acquainted with the strength and the weakness of the population among which he had spent his life, Curzio was for me an invaluable cicerone on the somewhat new ground on which I was treading. For if in my long sojourn abroad I had learned some things of foreign countries, I had also unlearned much about my own, which I had a very actual interest to learn again. And I must say that most of the information I gleaned from my friend was afterwards fully confirmed by subsequent personal experience. But to return to our vintage.

What with cutting grapes, and what with doing ample honour to an excellent dinner served on the grass, the day was on the wane before we knew where we were. Our Amphytrion, however, would not hear of our going home without my first seeing his *Uccel-*

liera. This was situated on a little eminence close by, perhaps a hundred paces above the vineyard in which we had been working—a spot famous for catching birds of passage. Catching birds of passage is a favourite sport, I ought rather to say a passion, with all classes in Italy, and it was with a treat of this kind that my friend intended to inaugurate the second and last day of my visit. An *Uccelliera* (fowling-box) I beg to explain, for the benefit of the uninitiated, is a small stone hut, the smaller the better, from the interior of which a person holding the cords attached to a double net outside, spreading in opposite directions, can at will, by a single twitch, bring the nets together, and thus envelope all the birds imprudent enough to have ventured within the circumjacent area. The amount of time, of patience, of labour, of ingenuity, which are lavished to lure and decoy the feathered tribe into the fatal snare is something astonishing. The juiciest berries which may tempt a bird out of its road hang from the shrubs all round the narrow enclosure, the choicest seeds strew the ground; caged birds hidden among the foliage (some barbarously blinded that they may sing at all seasons) call from their prison to their free brethren, while others, tied to one end of a short pole, are, by its being suddenly raised, set fluttering most invitingly. These and an infinity of other devices lie in wait for the winged wayfarers. The sport may be objected to on more grounds than one, but certainly not on that of want of excitement. I have seen grave senators pale with emotion at the approach of a flock of wild pigeons, cut capers at a happy catch, or be out of sorts all day at having missed a flight of linnets.

Feeling rather tired and heavy with my day's work, and having besides to get up betimes (the rendezvous at the *Uccelliera* was for five in the morning), I begged leave at about half-past nine in the evening to retire to my room, and I was in the act of going thither when a professional summons came for the Doctor to attend a woman in labour at some distance. In the uncertainty of how long he might be detained, perhaps the whole night, it was arranged between us, that if by four in the morning he had not come to call me, as previously agreed on, I should go by myself to the place of rendezvous. He would join me as soon as possible, and at all events I should find there some of the gentlemen with whom I had spent the day in the vineyard. Was I sure, quite sure, of being able to find my way alone to the *Uccelliera?* As sure as I was that I could find my way to bed.

My head was scarcely on my pillow when I fell asleep; and so sound was my slumber, that when I did awake, it was with a sense of having overslept myself. I lighted a match, and by its uncertain little flame I looked at my watch—ten minutes past four. Since Curzio had not come to rouse me, no doubt he had had to remain all night with his patient; so I rose, hurried on my clothes, stole softly down the stairs, lighted solely by my cigar, and glided out of the house. It was darker than the hour seemed to warrant, and at first I could scarcely see two steps before me; but this was only for a few moments. In proportion as I went along, so did the outlines of the neighbouring objects begin to shape themselves, though as yet dimly; the air was heavy and damp, not a star was visible. Nevertheless, the way to the *Uccelliera* was so easy—straight so far along the main road, and then to the right, through a lane dwindling to a path —that I could not have missed it if I would.

The fowling-box looked as if tenanted by Morpheus himself, so profoundly quiet was everything about it. To my surprise the door was shut, and yet it must necessarily have been close upon five o'clock. It was strange; but what was strangest of all was, that there should not be the slightest indication of incipient dawn in the east. I took out my watch, and—the mystery was explained. It was only a quarter to three! I had taken myself in famously. In my hurry and drowsiness I had mistaken the minute for the hour hand. What was I to do? Should I return to the house, and run the risk of rousing my hostess by knocking for admittance, or should I walk and smoke during the time to elapse before five? Now, it is one of my constitutional weaknesses to abhor inflicting unnecessary inconvenience on any of my friends, old or new, so I speedily determined in favour of the peripatetic process, and began leisurely to retrace the way I had come.

As I was nearing the lane abutting on the main road, it began to rain pretty fast. I knew of a place near at hand, for it had attracted my notice the day before, where I could find shelter, and I made for it at once. This was an arched recess in one of the walls of the lane above mentioned, having just room enough in it for a well breast-high with a stone seat behind it. The well had been abandoned, and was covered; it served now as a resting-place for peasants and their loads. The walls, or *muricciuoli*, which rose twice at least my height on each side, let but little light penetrate into this species of hole; enough though, after my eyes had had time to get accustomed to the obscurity, to discern the round shape of the well under my nose, and to have a faint perception that there stood opposite to me something more solid than air, which might well chance to be another wall, or *muricciuolo*. Having by this time finished my cigar, I crossed my arms, Napoleon-like, over my breast, shut my eyes, and asked myself if I could *bonâ fide* declare myself to be that identical individual who, but one short week ago, was buying Giusti's *Poesie*, at Truchy's, on the Boulevart des Italiens; and while I was considering the question, I felt touched by a magic wand,

and conveyed to the Boulevart aforesaid, where the first thing I saw was a patrol of soldiers bearing down on me with measured tread.

A sound of footsteps, not dreamed of this time, real footsteps of several persons reverberating through the narrow passage, fell upon my ear. They came from the heights, I mean from the side opposite to the town, and had somewhat of the regular tramp of soldiers, or funeral bearers. I strained my eyes—one, two, three—they passed me, but for the sound of their steps, like a spectral procession, slow, solemn, mute. The first, a little in advance of the others, carried what I surmised to be iron tools, from the jingling they made. Between the second and the third there was the length of something they bore upon their shoulders, and which accounted for the regular measure of their step—a something long and dark, save where it protruded beyond the back of the second bearer. This end, all wrapped in white, had a round fantastic shape, than which nothing could be more suggestive of a shrouded head. The illusion was so complete, that I could not repress a shudder, which, after a moment's reflection, was followed by a smile.

My curiosity, anyhow, was strongly excited. Where could they be going? What was it they were carrying? After all, might it not really be a corpse, the victim of some accident, being carried home by friends or neighbours? As I was thus cogitating, the footsteps stopped, to begin again almost immediately, but as it seemed to me, in another direction, and with less distinctness. I cautiously followed in their wake, and soon found myself at the foot of one of those rugged flights of stone steps which at every turn give access to the olive plantations of the Riviera; there I came to a stand, and listened. My mysterious trio had evidently gone up that way, for the echo of their feet came now, a little deadened, from above me. I went up three of the stone steps; the tramp ceased all at once, ten seconds of dead stillness, then the thump of something heavy dropped on the earth.

"Hush!" said a voice, reprovingly, "to work, and the quicker the better. Hist! what's that? somebody on the watch?"

It was only I, who in ascending another step had unwarily dislodged a loose stone, which had rolled down noisily. This fourth step had brought my eyes on a level with the adjacent ground, a flat square, and as far as I could see, thickly planted with trees. Strain my eyes as I would, I could distinguish nothing but a vista of trunks.

"Only some ferret," suggested a second voice, after a pause, employed, I fancy, in listening, and during which I had scarcely dared to breathe.

"More likely a fox," opined a third voice; "there is plenty of that vermin hereabouts."

"Let us hope so," resumed the first voice; "I would rather not be caught at this sort of business."

"Nor I"—"Nor I," assented the other two voices in succession. Although they spoke in whispers, I did not lose a syllable of what they said; but why should they speak in whispers?

Voice No. 1 made itself heard again. "This hole is not deep enough, dig deeper—softly." A spade was in motion instantly. The mention of a hole (*fossa*) had an ominous sound to my ears. A hole, and to bury what? One had evidently been prepared beforehand! What could this portend? Was I really on the track of some foul deed?

"There, that will do," said voice No. 1, and the sound of the spade ceased. "Where is the body? Bring it here."

The body! (*il morto!*) my hair stood on end.

The . . . thing for which he had asked was not brought but dragged to him. The lowering of it into the earth took long, and was attended by difficulty. I could hear the hard breathing of the men under the exertion; I could hear them moving about, and going to and fro in search of tools, as I supposed, to facilitate their task. At last it was accomplished, and nothing remained but to shovel in the earth. This was done quickly but cautiously, by three spades all working at once. Then there was the sound of the stamping of feet on the freshly-turned ground. A fiendish sneer from spokesman No. 1 crowned the horror of the scene. "We leave you in your snug berth; stay there in peace, and tell no tales." Such was the witty sally with which probably the murderer parted from his victim. It was received with suppressed laughter by the two wretches, his accomplices.

Thereupon they all left, two went up, the third down the hill at full gallop, and across the country in the direction of the town.

I stood transfixed as though spellbound for some minutes, and then I too set off as fast as I could back to my friend's house, harassed by a feeling impossible to describe. My hand was on the knocker, when the door opened, and a peasant issued forth. I asked him if the Doctor was at home. He said yes—adding something complimentary about my being so early a riser. Judge of the shock I got when I recognized the voice of the chief actor in the late drama! I looked the man full in the face. He struck me as having a most patibulary countenance, and I entered the house. Curzio, candle in hand, was at the top of the stairs. "Is that you?" "Yes, it is me." "Where the deuce do you come from, dripping wet, and with that haggard face?" "From witnessing a deed of darkness," I replied. "Nonsense—what do you mean?" and he stared at me in alarm. "Come to my room, and you shall hear," said I. And as soon as we were closeted, I told him my tale, told it with an emotion and conviction that were infectious. Poor Curzio looked like a ghost himself, as he thrust both hands into his hair, protesting vehemently and incoherently that it could not be, that I was the dupe of some hallucination.

"Would to God I were!" said I. "By-the-by, who is that man I met just now leaving the house?"

"That's Bastian, my bailiff, as trustworthy a fellow——"

"Your trustworthy fellow is a villain," cried I; "he was one of the three, and their chief."

This revelation had a queer and unexpected effect upon my friend. His fear-contracted features relaxed, his rigid mouth distended, and he burst forth into one of the most glorious laughs I ever heard from mortal lips. "My mulberries," he chuckled; "I see it all now, it is my mulberries."

It was my turn now to stare at him; and it took him some time to recover composure enough to give me the following explanation: "You must know that ever since the appearance of oidium, I have had it in my mind to try whether mulberry trees could or could not be grown with success on our slopes, but one thing or another obliged me to postpone the experiment. If we could add the produce of silkworms to that of our olives, it would be a great help to us in our years of bad crop or no crop at all. I must not forget to say that public feeling hereabouts is most opposed to the cultivation of mulberry trees: first, because it is a novelty, and consequently an abomination; secondly, on account of a certain local tradition, the origin of which has baffled all my researches. Once on a time, according to this tradition, the rearing of silkworms was the chief industry of these parts, and the women sufficing for the work, nothing was left for the men but to starve or emigrate. To argue about the absurdity of this last consequence would be like pounding water in a mortar—it is an article of faith with our folks. Well, a few days ago, I received from a friend of mine, a grower of mulberry trees in Piedmont, a sample of saplings, six in number, I believe, and I gave Bastian orders to plant them. He at first made a very wry face, and then, after a good deal of circumlocution, asked me if I should have any objection to his planting them by night. I inquired why at night rather than by day—I had of course guessed the reason. You shall have his answer in his own words; it is instructive in many ways. 'Why,' says he, 'if I put in these trees by day, and I am seen doing it, as I must be, I shall be a marked man for the rest of my life, which would be especially vexatious for me, who have both wife and children; whereas if I do it by night, and nobody sees me, nobody can fix the odium of the deed upon me, and suppose any one suspects me my No is as good as their Yes.' I granted his request, and thus it came to pass that the planting of my half-dozen young trees had to be accomplished as though it were a midnight crime."

Seen by the new light thrown upon them by Curzio's explanation, the features of the case lost their phantasmagoric halo, and resumed their natural appearance. The shrouded head was but the roots of the saplings tied together with a cloth to preserve the native earth adhering to them; the body (*il morto*) was but a commonly used Italian figure of speech to denote anything the object of some mystery (the saplings in our case), the same as saying a "dead secret;" Bastian's fiendish sneer was only an innocent joke far from inappropriate to the circumstance; his patibulary countenance a freak of my heated fancy, etc. etc. And so nothing remained, save a little laugh at its discoverer, of the Deed of Darkness.

END OF "A DEED OF DARKNESS."

A MODEST CELEBRITY.

A MODEST CELEBRITY.

Some years ago I set out to visit Italy for the first time, and took my way up the Rhine and through Switzerland. A lady friend whom I was to meet, with her family at Milan, had desired me to bring her some of Jean Maria Farina's true and genuine eau de Cologne; and anxious, like a true knight, to fulfil the behest of lady fair, no sooner was I arrived at Cologne, and the duties of the toilet and my breakfast were over, than I sallied out to execute my commission. I had not taken twenty steps along the street, when, over a warehouse door, a large board struck my eye, thus inscribed in gigantic capitals—

ONLY VERITABLE AGENT FOR THE SALE OF
JEAN MARIA FARINA'S GENUINE EAU DE COLOGNE.

This was just what I wanted. The shop contained nothing but bottles of eau de Cologne, for the most part neatly packed by dozens in slight wooden boxes. I made my purchase, desired the box to be carried to the hotel, and went forth to take a survey of the town. But I had not proceeded many steps further, before another sign-board made precisely the same pretensions for its shop, as being the sole depositary of the genuine eau de Cologne by Jean Maria Farina. I was startled. "I hope I have made no mistake," thought I. "If I have, it must be rectified: there is full time."

Vexed at my precipitancy, I walked on thoughtfully, and soon came to another, and another, and another warehouse of the same description; and so on, in every part of the town, all bearing, in every diversity of colour and characters, the same announcement of being "the sole and veritable depositary of Jean Maria Farina's genuine eau de Cologne." I made anxious inquiries of divers persons, without arriving at anything satisfactory; and so, returning to my hotel, I determined to abide by my purchase, and to present it to my fair friend as the real and genuine eau de Cologne, without disturbing her faith by the doubts that distracted my own mind. The subject vanished gradually from my thoughts, only leaving behind it a general impression of the greatness of Jean Maria Farina, that European personage, whose name had stared me thus in the face at every turn in the old town on the Rhine.

Next morning I set off for Mainz by the steamboat. The vessel was crowded with passengers, of whom the majority were English. To own the truth, I am apt to feel greatly ashamed of my countrymen —speaking of them in the mass—when I meet them abroad, swarming in steamboats, railways, and hotels.

On this occasion my eye wandered over the commonplace set, with their endless and cumbersome abundance of travelling comforts in the shape of bags, baskets, bottles, and boxes of all sizes and forms. There were likewise flat-faced Germans, smoking extraordinary pipes, and wearing fantastical hats and caps; but of the whole crowd, the only individual who at all fixed my attention was a tall man somewhat advanced in years, and his black hair sprinkled with white, though he was still of comely appearance. The deep-set black eyes, olive complexion, oval-shaped head, and finely-cut features, the mobility and *finesse* of expression, the pliable and easy motions of the body, stamped him a native of the south. There was a shrewd thoughtfulness in the countenance while silent, brightening when he spoke into benevolent cheerfulness, a good-humoured smile lighting his dark eyes, and disclosing a fine set of white teeth, which gave something very agreeable to the whole physiognomy. He looked like a prosperous man, well contented with himself and with the world. That his prosperity had been *earned*, seemed denoted by an appearance of activity which age had not subdued.

The old gentleman was surrounded by a numerous party, and nothing occurred to bring about any communication between us. But by an odd chance we happened to meet every day for a week either in a steamboat, on a railway, or at a *table-d'hôte*—always at a distance, however, without at any time exchanging a word. There was a sort of silent acquaintance established, but we seemed under a spell which obliged us to look, and not to speak. At last it was with a kind of painful consciousness our eyes met, although feeling rather attracted than repelled; so that it was almost a relief the first day I no longer met my dark-eyed vision at supper, although I felt, notwithstanding, a lingering regret that I should now never satisfy a certain curiosity which had sprung up in my own mind as to who or what the stranger might be.

I stayed some time in Switzerland, and then went on to Italy. I crossed the Alps by the Simplon—that wonderful road conceived by the genius of Napoleon—as easy as an English turnpike-road, winding its way up through mountain pastures and vast pine forests to the regions of eternal snow and ice, and the wild territory of the avalanche. Nothing gives a more forcible impression of the power of man's intellect, struggling, calmly and successfully, with the awful powers of nature. Arrived at the summit of the pass, the descent on the Italian side begins from the village of Simplon; and you go winding down, between gigantic, perpendicular, larch-grown rocks, which seem to admit reluctantly within their jaws the road that winds along the edge of the roaring torrent, which has fretted its way during long ages through these rocky walls. Road and torrent run together confined between them, and the traveller sees the sky far above the towering masses on either side.

After passing several hours in this gorge, you issue from it suddenly, where at your feet lies, opening to view, the verdant, smiling basin of the Val d'Ossola, rich in luxuriant Italian beauty. After the stern grandeur of the Alpine pass, the view from the bridge of Crevola bursts like enchantment on the sight, presenting a wide, gracefully-circular plain, watered by a winding river, and surrounded by the most picturesque mountains, clothed half-way up their sides with rich wood, while above stand out the naked, brown mountain-tops in fantastic peaks against the blue sky. Among the dark verdure of their swelling base stand forth in strong relief cheerful white villages and country-houses, and tall square white church towers, spotting the sides of the hills, while the town of Domo d'Ossola shines smilingly at the further end of the vale. The vine, allowed to run in its elegant natural festoons, the mulberry mixed with other trees, and the soft balmy air, all tell the traveller he has set foot in Italy. Domo d'Ossola struck me as a cheerful, elegant little town. It had an Italian character, quite new to me, which took my fancy. I travelled alone, guided solely by my own inclination; and I was so much pleased with the situation, that I determined to give some days to examine a few of the numerous valleys which diverge from the Val d'Ossola, winding among these picturesque, but rarely-explored mountains.

I have always had a passion for deviating from the high road. After resting a night at Domo, I inquired if a guide could be procured. My host informed me that as few travellers wandered from the high road, there were no regular guides, but that there was at that moment in his house a young man, servant to a gentleman of the Val Vegeste, who was returning to Santa Maria Maggiore, the principal village in that valley, whom I could accompany thus far. Arrived there, I might easily find some one else to guide me further on. The arrangement was soon made; and Battistino—so my guide was named—and I set out on foot together towards the Val Vegeste. My companion was a barefooted, tall, active, black-eyed, intelligent young fellow, with those free and supple limbs, and that somewhat melancholy cast of countenance—easily, however, brightening into an animated and cheerful variety of expression—which characterise the Italian peasant.

I knew something of the Italian language, but I was totally at a loss to communicate with my present conductor, whose only tongue was his native mountain dialect, in which I with difficulty recognised here and there some word disfigured by a pronunciation wholly new to me; so our communication was more in looks and gestures than in speech. We first retraced a short part of the road by which I had entered the town the day before; but soon deviating to the right, we crossed by a plank bridge the stream which intersects the Val d'Ossola, and proceeding to the limit of the valley in that direction, and then turning to the left, skirted the base of the mountain. Nothing could exceed the beauty of everything that met my eye. After an hour's walk, I was struck by the appearance of a very handsome country-house, which stood on a lofty eminence facing us, surrounded by noble terraced gardens. The mansion commanded the same extensive views of the beautiful valley that strike the traveller so forcibly from the bridge of Crevola. I pointed out this dwelling to my guide with an inquiring look.

"Palazzo del Signor Padrone" ("The palace of my master") was his answer.

"Your padrone then is rich?"

"Hu!" returned Battistino with a lengthened exclamation, waving his hand expressively up and down. "Tanto ricco!—ricchissimo! Tanto scior!" ("So rich! —very rich! Such a great gentleman!") And this was followed by a long and eloquent eulogium, or history, unfortunately lost upon me, with the exception of the words, "Generoso, generosissimo—da Paris," by which I made out the very rich man to be likewise very generous, and to have come from Paris.

As we proceeded along our way, I found that we were not to go towards the palace, as Battistino termed the handsome dwelling upon the hill, our road turning sharp to the right, where a singularly picturesque opening gives entrance to the wild Val Vegeste. Here we crossed a bridge over a beautiful stream, flowing from between two high walls of rock, richly grown with overhanging wood. A few houses stand on this spot, and a chapel with an image of the Virgin, to which is attached a legendary miracle; and from thence a road cut in the rock leads up the course of the stream to Santa Maria Maggiore. At every step the picturesque beauties of this singular valley become more striking. As we advanced, the sound of a fine-toned church-bell came wafted on the air. It sounded like a rejoicing peal. Battistino became excited, and contrived to make me understand that the bell, the *great* bell, was a gift from his padrone to the church.

On entering Santa Maria Maggiore, we found the whole village in holiday trim: the women's heads adorned with snow-white muslin handkerchiefs, or braids of hair fastened round the back of the head by large silver pins placed in a semicircle—the latter coiffure having a peculiarly classical and Italian appearance. Some added coquettishly a natural flower on one side. Their ears and necks were adorned with large earrings and necklaces; and the neat stocking, and embroidered instep of a sort of slipper, with a wooden sole and heels, under a short smart petticoat, completed the holiday attire. Each, with fan in hand, was hurrying to church; while some, after a fashion peculiar to these mountains, carried their infants attached to their backs in light wooden cradles.

The whole formed a rich and novel scene. My guide had a word, a nod, or a smile for everybody, and you may suppose that the stranger with him excited no slight attention. Battistino seemed irresistibly impelled to follow the crowd, and led me with him into the church. We walked up a side aisle, and he pointed out from afar the altar-piece, with a gesture which implied that he looked upon it as a masterpiece of art, whispering at the same time, "Gift of the padrone." As I perceived the eyes of the congregation fixed upon me, I was going to propose that we should leave the church, when a numerous company entering, relieved me from the attention of the congregation, and I remained a forgotten observer. The new-comers were two young couples, surrounded by their respective friends, coming to the altar to receive the nuptial benediction.

"Pepino and Ghita, Giovanni and Maria," said my guide in an undertone, as he pointed out the couples; and he went on to make me understand that his padrone had given the dota (marriage-portion.) His enthusiasm now seemed to lose all power of expression in words, and to concentrate itself in his two bright eyes; while I thought to myself: "This padrone of his must be a rare character—a rich and liberal man dispensing his wealth in shedding happiness among the simple population of this retired valley. I should like to see him."

The wedding-party had stopped in the middle of the church, as if waiting for some one; a moment after, the expected person made his appearance. "Il padrone!" exclaimed Battistino; and at the same instant I recognised my old mysterious acquaintance of the steamboat.

The priest now stood at the altar, the marriage-ceremony was performed, and the blessing given. The two wedding-parties walked out of the church to return to their respective homes. At the door of the church, all crowded round Battistino's master with various expressions of affectionate and respectful gratitude, which he received with fatherly good-humour, and then disengaged himself from the group. His eye had caught mine, and we exchanged a smile of recognition. Battistino darted forward, and said a few words to him; after which the stranger moved towards me, and accosting me with courteous ease in good French, said, that since fate seemed determined to procure him the pleasure of my acquaintance, I must allow him to look upon a foreigner, who did this remote valley the very rare honour of a visit, as his welcome guest. I was too well pleased with the invitation to hesitate in accepting the hospitality offered with so good a grace, and so benevolent a smile; and had I acceded less readily, a sudden clap of thunder, and the bursting of an unexpected storm over our heads, would have left me little choice: as it was, I was made doubly grateful.

I followed my new friend into the open door of a handsome house, while sudden night seemed to occupy the place of day; and the rain poured down in torrents, making me appreciate such comfortable shelter. My host was cordially and gracefully courteous. He assured me that the streams and torrents, swollen by the rain, would make it impossible to proceed in the direction I had intended; and that even when the storm abated, it would already have cut off my return to Domo; for the small stream I had crossed by a plank in the morning must now be swollen, by innumerable mountain-tributaries, into a wide, deep, and impassable torrent. He therefore begged me to submit with patience to necessity, and allow him to make me his guest for the night. He had come that morning from the country-house I had perhaps remarked before entering Val Vegeste, for the purpose of being present at the two marriages that had taken place, and purposed returning as soon as the rain cleared off. He added, that at Monte Christesi he should have the pleasure of introducing me to his wife and family. So, as soon as the storm rolled away, and a blue sky once more smiled upon the valley, Battistino brought to the door a four-wheeled open carriage drawn by one horse; he mounted the front seat as driver, and my host and I took our places behind.

We rolled along the rocky road I had followed on foot. Battistino pointed to the road, and said something to me, of which the word "padrone" was the only one I understood. I turned to my host for an explanation. He said, laughing, "Battistino is anxious to inform you that this road from Santa Maria Maggiore to Domo was made by me: some years ago there was only a bridle-path. Living in the neighbourhood, I was of course one of the most interested in the improvement."

Battistino turned again to add some words on the subject. At the same instant, we came to a sharp turn in the road; and as our driver's eye was not upon his horse, we ran full against a car laden with hay drawn by an ox. The wheels locked, and that of our vehicle gave way, and came off. We got out of the carriage, leaving the mortified Battistino to remedy the damage, and follow in the best way he could. As we walked on, we were overtaken by two youths, each with a pack on his back, and a staff over his shoulder, with a pair of thick-soled shoes slung upon it. They went the swift noiseless gliding pace of the barefooted Italian peasant. My host exchanged kind salutations with the lads, and bade them go on to his house, where they should sleep that night, as the swollen state of the torrents would not let them proceed farther;

and he added: "To-morrow morning I will give you a letter which may be of use to you." He then desired them to go on before us, and announce that he was following with a stranger gentleman.

My host then explained to me that these youths were leaving home to seek their fortunes abroad, their native valleys being too poor to maintain their population. A large portion of the males emigrate, and generally return at the end of a few months with the little earnings they have gained in some distant place by their industry; then, after a while, they go forth again, like bees to gather new honey. Their traffic is chiefly in tin-ware, or in simples, of which these mountains offer an abundant supply. During the absence of the men, the women and children cultivate the poor soil.

"Our Italians," continued the padrone, "are an intelligent race, full of resources, and generally succeed in what they undertake. A most erroneous impression prevails with respect to us in other countries. In my travels I have constantly heard of the idleness of the Italian peasantry—of the '*dolce far niente*' of Italy. Yet there is no country in which the peasantry labour so incessantly, and with so much intelligence, activity, and cheerful industry. I can vouch for so much at least to the credit of Lombardy and Piedmont, which I know intimately. If you, sir, were to remain long enough in this country, to have opportunities of observing our rural life, you would soon be convinced of this. No part of the world is more travelled by foreigners, and so little known. But if strangers underrate our country, most of its wandering sons hold it in loving remembrance. I have myself been absent many long years, and have seen many lands, but I never forgot this spot. I left it, fifty years ago, a poor mountain boy, like those you saw just now, and I always said in my heart, 'If ever I can build a house, it shall be on Monte Christesi.' I never changed my mind, and there stands my house to-day. Never did I forget my love for these valleys." And as we advanced, he pointed out the different striking beauties of the prospect.

Everything I heard and saw served to heighten my curiosity respecting my companion, and I was framing in my mind some proper mode of shaping a few questions, when we arrived at the mansion. Here my host introduced me to his wife, a French lady, to two children, and to his brother. I immediately recognised the party in the steamboat. I was cordially received by all, almost as an old acquaintance, and the incidents of our unexpected meeting afforded subject of cheerful conversation. We sat down to dinner in a very handsome hall, ornamented, after the Italian manner, with fresco paintings on the walls and ceiling. Easy chat, and several bottles of good wine, rendered the meal very pleasant. After dinner, we passed from the dining-room to one of the garden-terraces, where coffee was served in the open air.

The terrace on which we were overlooked several others, shelving in succession to the limits of the property. The valley, enclosed by mountains, and watered by a rushing stream, was spread at our feet. The prospect was splendid; the sky glowed with the tints of the evening sun; and the late rain brought out in exquisite freshness the aromatic scent of the flowers and of the neighbouring woods.

It was a moment in which the heart opens to warm and easy sympathies. I felt no difficulty in asking my host to explain to me by what uncommon fortunes he had become, from a poor mountain boy, such as we had met in the morning, the happy possessor of so noble a property, and the benefactor of all around him.

He nodded with a shrewd and cheerful smile, saying, "I often wonder at it myself. You must know that in my travels I met with a magician who pointed the way to a golden fountain. I will tell you my modest history.

"I was born in Santa Maria Maggiore, the village you visited this morning. My parents were not so poor as the rest of the inhabitants, for my father, according to the custom I mentioned to you, had gone into foreign parts. My mother, too, accompanied him; and at the end of some years, they had collected, by their industry in managing a humble commerce, that which was a little fortune on their return to their native vale. They possessed a field more than their neighbours, and two cows to fill the double office of supplying the family with milk and drawing the plough —as you see that cow doing yonder, guided by a woman and a girl. Yet when the family increased, and three boys grew into lads, the means of the family could not suffice for our maintenance. I was the eldest, and while yet in tender years, it became necessary for me to follow the course of most of our valesmen, and go to earn a living elsewhere.

"My parents had carried on their little trade in simples in a town upon the Rhine, and they gave me a letter of recommendation to a friend and distant connection, a chemist and druggist there. With this letter, a few pieces of money in my pocket, and a pack on my back, I set out for a foreign land—distant in reality, and still more so in my imagination. The fancy of youth is always excited by the thought of travel, adventure, and independence, and my spirits kept up well till the day of departure, when the awfulness of separation from all I loved came with full force upon my heart. In those days there were no steamboats or railways—nothing to reduce distance, or ease the toils of the poor traveller. On foot, or with some occasional lift from a slow-going vehicle, or some floating raft, was I to wend my way to my remote destination. I shall never forget the day of my departure. My mother accompanied me as far as the chapel of the Madona you saw this morning. On that spot we parted with many tears. Before our last embrace, my mother knelt before the image of the Virgin, and I beside her, to implore a blessing on my adventure. Then my mother hung round my neck her own rosary. 'Keep this, my son,' she said, 'in memory of your mother. Be a good boy, and never forget your prayers. Every evening I shall say a pater and an ave for you. Now, my boy, farewell! God bless you!'

"I have this rosary still. Sad, indeed, did I feel that night when the melancholy tinkling of the Ave Maria bell sounded from a distant village where I was to rest, and which I hastened to reach before the twilight should deepen into night. How often, through many long years, at the sound of the evening bell, did my sinking heart yearn for my mother and my home!

"Well, in due time I reached my destination, presented the letter to the protector to whom my parents had directed me, and was taken into his service. He was an intelligent man, with an inventive turn of mind, which he applied to the practical purpose of improving his business by the sale of certain mixtures, of which he alone possessed the secret. He was of a capricious disposition, and often became disgusted with his assistants. To me, however, he took a fancy, and proved invariably kind. He initiated me into the mysteries of the laboratory sufficiently to enable me to be of real use in his operations; but he carefully kept some mysterious secrets to himself: praising, nevertheless, my intelligence, activity, and zeal, and becoming more and more attached to me. I was of a cheerful disposition, and my lively sallies and ingenuous remarks amused and cheered the old man. But while I imparted vivacity to his age, my own spirits gradually sunk under the influence of a total change of life—shut up as I was in a dismal laboratory, behind a dark shop, in a narrow street, instead of roaming among our beautiful valleys and breezy mountains. My natural buoyancy bore me up for a time; but as month after month, and even year after year, rolled on in the same monotony, I sunk into unconquerable depression. All surrounding objects became disgusting to me; the very quality of the air, and colour of the light, grew odious. Day and night I was haunted by the thought of the immeasurable distance I had traversed, and which divided me from home. The familiar faces and sounds of my native scenes gleamed upon me in waking dreams. The best moment of the day was when the bell of the Ave Maria brought to my lips my mother's prayer, and to my eyes a refreshing shower of tears.

"Three years had elapsed since my departure from home, when these impressions reached their greatest intensity. My gains were small, and part I had already sent to my family. I thought with agony that not only I had no store by me, but that I had not even sufficient to take me home. I felt as if I must die an outcast in a distant land. My strength failed rapidly, and at last I was obliged to take to my bed. My master consulted a medical man who often came to our shop. He examined me, and pronounced my malady to be no other than nostalgia. The only remedy was to revisit my native land. My worthy master proved himself truly kind; not only did he allow me three months' holidays to go home, but he advanced me the sum necessary for the journey, undertaken of course in the most economical way. He gave me, besides, a letter to my parents, expressive of his satisfaction with my conduct and abilities, and likewise of his desire for my return to his service.

"From that moment he obtained my unbounded gratitude and attachment. No sooner was this plan settled, than my spirits rose, and life seemed infused into my veins. In a few days I was able to rise from my bed of sickness, and set forth on my way homewards. At the first sight of my native valley, at the first breath of the mountain-breezes, at the first embrace of my father, mother, and brothers, all my ills vanished, and health and strength returned to me, as if wafted on the very air. I was speedily quite recovered. I spent a happy three months at home, and then set out to return to my kind old master with renewed courage, instead of the hopeless feeling of banishment. Now I went with the firm hope and resolve to return again, as my parents had done before me, with my modest gains, and settle in this spot, the dearest to me on earth. I trusted that a few years' exertion could accomplish this. I was animated also by a desire to prove my gratitude to my benevolent master, and I came back to his service with redoubled zeal. By degrees he initiated me into many delicate operations, and instructed me in the choice and preparation of various simples, which he often sent me on long excursions to collect. These he prepared for divers uses. His confidence in me increased, on finding that I never pressed inquiries on any point upon which he wished to maintain reserve. Each year the good old man grew more attached to me. He had no near relative of his own; I became to him as a son, and I endeavoured to fulfil the duties of one. Age crept on, with its infirmities; he felt life drawing to a close; and calling me to his bedside, he ordered me to take down in writing certain notes he dictated—the secret, as he termed it, of the golden fountain. 'Your activity and ingenuity,' said he, 'will follow out these hints so as to lead you to it infallibly, my dear child. I may well call you so, for you have been an affectionate child to me.'

"Not long afterwards I followed my adopted father to the grave. He had bequeathed to me all his possessions. They were very humble; but I perceived that in his last instructions, if judiciously improved, he had indeed opened a road which might lead to fortune. The course pointed out shortly led me to Paris, where, without giving up my establishment on the banks of the Rhine, I opened another for the sale of genuine and improved eau de Cologne, by Jean Maria Farina."

"Do I then stand," exclaimed I, rising with a feeling of enthusiasm and reverence, "in the presence of that celebrated man? Truly I thank my fortune for having guided me so agreeably to the gratification of a strong desire in so pleasant a meeting!" My host was flattered and amused at this burst, and laughed much at the description I gave him of my perplexity at Cologne in trying to find out his real establishment.

"'Tis true," replied he, "it stands in a very obscure corner of an old narrow street. I never left the old Ulick's Platz: I never abandoned the original establishment of my friend." Our conversation then diverged to other interesting points, and my host added a few details, which completed his autobiography.

Eau de Cologne has been to him truly an Aladdin's lamp—a magic cruise. The sale rapidly brought him a fortune. Jean Maria early visited a second time his native place, and had the happiness to lavish on his parents more comforts and luxury than had ever even entered their dreams. They dwelt long in Santa Maria Maggiore, proud and happy in their son's prosperity. He never forgot his love for his native valley, and has invested part of his property in the purchase of land in the Val Vegeste and its neighbourhood. He built the mansion, and laid out the gardens on Monte Christesi, where he now received me, and where he has settled one of his brothers. His wife is French, and he has several children. He contributes with generous care to the welfare of the poor in his neighbourhood. He knows intimately their wants and their feelings; and is therefore competent, from experience as well as inclination, to dispense, with the best effect, his munificence among those who want his assistance.

He constantly spends the winter in Paris, and the summer in his native home among the folds of the Alps, much loved by all around. I slept that night under the hospitable roof of Monte Christesi; and my kind host and I parted next morning with the promise of meeting again.

Ever since then, Eau de Cologne is associated in my mind with the ancient cathedral town beside the Rhine—the romantic Val Vegeste and Val d'Ossola—the mansion on Monte Christesi — and the uncommon fortunes, European name, and goodly benevolent presence of Jean Maria Farina.

THE END.

www.ingramcontent.com/pod-product-compliance
Lightning Source LLC
Chambersburg PA
CBHW052213240426
43670CB00037B/431

9783742806864